FINDING HOME

BY ANNE AYERS KOCH

Finding Home

A MEMOIR OF ARTS AND CRAFTS

by Anne Ayers Koch

LUMINARE PRESS

EUGENE, OREGON

Finding Home: A Memoir of Arts and Crafts
© 2012 Anne Ayers Koch

Printed in the United States of America

Cover Design: Claire Flint, Three Seed Design

Luminare Press
467 W 17th Ave
Eugene, OR 97401
www.luminarepress.com

LCCN: 2012947488

ISBN: 978-1-937303-05-1

Out of the
chaos
the imagination
frames a
thing of beauty

—John Livingston Lowe

For Jim

We built it together

Mid pleasures and palaces though we may roam,
Be it ever so humble, there's no place like home;
A charm from the skies seems to hallow us there,
Which, seek through the world, is ne'er met with elsewhere.
—J.H. Payne, 1823

Table of Contents

PREFACE

The small box, with its geometric inlaid light and dark pattern, was a gift from my father after one of his Navy deployments. When he pulled it from his duffle bag I tried to hide my disappointment. It looked like a decorated wooden rectangle. I had been hoping for a Japanese doll, or maybe a jewelry box. "What could it be?" I wondered.

"It opens," he smiled. "It's a puzzle. See if you can solve it."

After several days and many broad hints from Dad, I figured out by pushing and pulling the delicate wood design that the box unfolded to reveal a tiny drawer. It became the destination for treasures— delicate seashells, colored stones, jaunty acorn caps, shiny coins retrieved from couch cushions.

I grew older. The world grew more complicated, more strident, harder to understand. The box became a way of thinking about the challenges we all face on the other side of childhood—homemaking, parenting, shaping time beyond the ring of school bells. Most of my answers came from books. But not all of them.

Facing those challenges was like unlocking the box—frustrating—no instructions provided. Through a process of trial and error—touching, shaking, looking from different angles—I found the secret lever. One step led to the next. The box grew bigger. More appealing. More beautiful than its surface design suggested. Life is the same.

There are those who don't consider crafts and porcelain painting art—dismissed as the product of technicians or "mere" illustrators. They are art—art for everyone, not just the wealthy or intellectual elite. Society thinks art needs intermediaries. It isn't important if the public understands it. Even worse if they like it. Oscar Wilde captured the idea. "Art should never try to be popular. The public should try to make itself artistic."

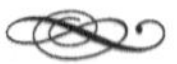

My adventures with crafts and painting led me to an insight I might have otherwise missed. There are all kinds of stories to tell. Most use words, but some do not. The tools I chose and the projects woven through the decades have been simple ones. But in their ordinariness something happened. The dilemmas, disappointments, discoveries, and often, the delights that have surprised me have been easier to understand, as ideas that belonged to the arts became ideas for living.

Beginning a craft project or opening my paint box feels like entering C.S. Lewis's magic wardrobe. Other worlds appear. They are colorful places, teeming with possibilities. They are places where choices often lead to unanticipated outcomes—sometimes worse, more often better.

Alvin Toffler observed in *The Third Wave* that to create a fulfilling emotional life and sane emerging civilization for tomorrow, people need three basic requirements: community, structure, and meaning. I disagree. It isn't only the future that needs those things. We have always needed ways to transform life from a box with no exit, to a place where dreams and discoveries make living a deeper, richer, wider journey.

I was an unsuitable candidate for the kingdoms that make up art and design. Yet with no formal training at the outset, and no apparent aptitude, the time I have spent "thinking" with my hands…painting, printing, creating from scraps and castoffs, have sent shafts of light across countless murky hours.

Set against the backdrop of my decisions to explore old-fashioned crafts, and later, porcelain painting, the essays here are a tribute to my journey with art—its influence and its unexpected lessons.

There are lots of ways to open a box. Art is one.

Part One

Energy Unbridled

"*The real essence of work is concentrated energy.*"
—Walter Begehot

WHEN WORDS AREN'T ENOUGH

Draw. Decorate. Design. All were outside my sturdy middle-class school experience. In a curriculum where memorization and outlining were daily companions, art was an infrequent visitor...and never for a "serious" student. I was a serious student.

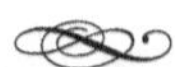

The Space Age began October 4, 1957, when the USSR launched Sputnik I, the first earth-orbiting satellite. In case we weren't intimidated enough, that same year Soviets also tested the first ICBM, a self-propelled unmanned missile capable of carrying nuclear warheads. The country riveted its attention on the "space race"...a race that focused schools on "important subjects"—science, math, civics. There was little room for art. Americans were busy building concrete bomb shelters in their backyards while peering skyward—positive missiles would be raining down any minute. My classmate, Karen, had the nicest bunker in the city. We all wanted to be her friend.

Lillian J. Rice Elementary School, where I began fifth grade that year, sits in the southwest corner of Chula Vista, then a sleepy town eight miles north of the Mexican border. Built in 1938, it had three

1

single-story wings of self-contained classrooms clustered like domi-
noes at right angles to one another. At the far edge of the property
squatted two rectangular portables the same dusty color as the playground. On the first day of school our new teacher, a slight, timid
man who wore a dark wool suit that day and every day after (despite
the hot southern California fall weather), couldn't get the noise level
below deafening. As 3 o'clock approached he made an announcement.

We were curious. The room fell silent. It is the singular quiet
moment I recall. Longer recess? No homework? The suit should
have tipped us off. The quiet disconcerted him. Twisting his hands
like someone demonstrating the best way to use hand sanitizer, he
told us art and music would be our "reward" at the end of each week.
Why? Because we were "stuck" in one of the dilapidated temporary
classrooms.

Murmurs began to percolate as he rushed on. He explained he
would bring symphonic music to play on the record player perched
atop the dented gray file cabinet behind his desk. The clincher:
while we listened we could draw. We were unimpressed. We didn't
feel "stuck." We liked our classroom. We liked being away from the
"little kids." We liked the playground right outside the door. We didn't
know what symphonies were and weren't interested in finding out.

Every Friday Mr. Chang arrived, a large black vinyl record in a
paper jacket tucked under his arm. Every Friday chaos ensued. The
boys drew insulting pictures on their construction paper, then tore
them into tiny pieces for spit wad wars. The girls drew hearts and
played "hangman." Soon after Sputnik, art and music disappeared.
By Christmas the teacher disappeared as well after an unfortunate
incident. He somehow ended up stuck in the ball box while we snaked
around the room in a jerky conga line in time with a Beethoven
overture. Art education was over.

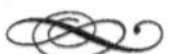

I threw myself into a tracked curriculum dominated by words… lab manuals, grammar tomes, foreign language workbooks, anthologies. Seven years later I found myself a freshman at Whittier College. Studying in the library one hot, smoggy afternoon, surrounded by piles of books and feeling the world was a huge fragmented set of competing ideas, I longed to look at something besides lines of text.

The bookstore was selling tiny books of famous art prints on a table by the checkout stand—twenty-five cents apiece. Without much thought I bought one. Rummaging through my book bag, I plucked it out. On the cover a red violin floated over the title: "Raoul Dufy—Music."

Flipping through the 4-inch prints, a stray thought pushed toward the surface like a swimmer coming up from a deep dive. I realized both my education and my heart had been missing something. Something important. Artists and craftsmen look for the same unity beneath life's disconcerting rumblings as do philosophers and writers. Different mediums. Similar goals.

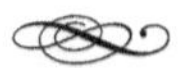

I went back to the bookstore and bought one copy of every pamphlet on the table. I stood them side-by-side around the wide library carrel desktop like baseball players looking from the dugout toward the playing field. When I tired of unraveling philosophical arguments or slogging through Randall's *Making of the Modern Mind*, the abstruse required text for the college's two-year *History of Western Civilization* course, I would disappear into one of the miniature pictures.

A door cracked open. I wandered through some of the world's great paintings and handcrafts. Pausing often to study some captivating detail, I recognized although the works were wildly different they had one thing in common. Artists work in multiple mediums… paint, marble, porcelain, wood, clay, fibers, photography, found objects, and more… because there are no words for what they want to convey. I spent two years at Whittier. The little art books were part of every day.

Towards the end of E.M. Forster's *A Room with a View*, the heroine, Lucy, expresses her debt to old Mr. Emerson. "It was as if he had made her see the whole of everything at once." I know now it is impossible to see the whole of even any one picture at once, let alone everything. But there was a single moment, long ago in the old wooden college library, where turning my eyes from the book before me to the art around me, I sensed for an instant that perhaps, just perhaps, everything might form a whole, at the edge of awareness in a place we seldom go.

These days I never look for missiles in the sky. I look instead at lights and shadows overhead, underfoot, all around. I look at my paint palette too.

The colors start out separated, lined up in anticipation of some project. Soon the palette is messy—colors oozing into one another, unexpected different hues percolating out. More interesting. More exuberant. Wholeness. Waiting to be found.

Once more.

> *"They cannot scare me with their empty spaces*
> *Between stars—on stars where no human race is.*
> *I have it in me so much nearer home*
> *To scare myself with my own desert places."*
> —Robert Frost

Empty Spaces

Now what?

First house. First job. The house was in an almost new tract miles from charming homes we couldn't afford around the university. The job matched Jim's research interests in business and labor relations. He had his hands full at work unraveling the Byzantine mysteries of academic communities.

At home I faced my own mysteries. Far from the crowded Los Angeles landscape we left, the house was a one story three-bedroom rectangle with a triangular roof pitch jutting over the front door, interrupting the flat elevation like a droopy umbrella.

The painter used two colors. The exterior was pale beige; the interior a collection of Navajo white walls, white metal closet doors, white window frames. Inside reminded me of a person trying hard not to be noticed in a crowd; the outside, of KOA campground tent signs jutting above highway billboard advertisements.

Tucked in Oregon's Willamette Valley, it sat midway on a street where every third house looked like ours. The interstate winding through the northwest was lined with towering Douglas firs. The unfortunate sparse neighborhood saplings were anemic cousins.

Standing in the vacant rooms, I thought of Willa Cather's pioneer stories of life on the Nebraska plains. In a wild leap I imagined myself on an empty road like the one in the Jules Breton painting *Song of the Lark* Cather used as the title of her 1915 story of a woman seeking a more artistic life. My quest wasn't so grand but the road was unfamiliar. Where should I begin? Looking for a way to soften the white box in which we found ourselves. Looking for a meaningful life outside the formal workplace I had left. Looking for ways to soothe the fatigue and insecurity of new parenthood.

It wasn't a question of being busy. That's easy. Yet activity, no matter how layered and intense, doesn't guarantee keeping emptiness at bay. Sometimes just the opposite.

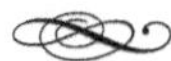

I found an answer in a Eugene library display for a brand new publication, *Early American Life*. A cross between an academic journal and magazine, it announced its intention to devote itself to stories featuring architecture, decorative arts, period style, and social history from colonial times to the mid-nineteenth century. Every issue featured homes, antiques, histories of crafts, biographies of forgotten Americans, heritage plants, and all things devoted to a "traditional, comfortable, warm sense" of America.

Traditional. Comfortable. Warm. It was a start. I subscribed and devoured every issue. Formatted in tiny print in two narrow columns, I poured through not just stories of how our ancestors had gone about creating homes and communities, but instructions for projects they undertook. *Early American Life* was the unlikely catalyst I needed to begin making sense of a new life chapter. Thoreau was right when he said, "How many a man has dated a new era in his life from the reading of a book?"

Many topics I dismissed—blacksmithing, using lye for soap making, woodcarving, plant propagation, recreating Martha Washington's Christmas dinner. Others looked intriguing...pinecone wreaths, cornhusk ornaments, rag dolls, cranberry garlands. I tried them all.

Bookbinding was first.

Our blue-collar neighbors and the young academics we socialized with thought such pursuits were unnecessary, even frivolous. Who cared about old time-consuming arts when modern life made buying everything, including books, as easy as shopping?

I cared, more than I thought I would at the start. And besides, look what shopping has done to us.

I remembered a phrase my high school French teacher used when we complained about his tedious assignments. Squaring his shoulders he would quote dramatically from Voltaire's 1736 *Le Mondain*—"Le superflu, chose tres necessaire." The superfluous is very necessary.

The trick is figuring out what is superfluous. None of us imagined paper books would become needless for many people before the next century was a decade old. Today we are awash in eReaders, Nooks, Kindles, iPads. At the same time scientists tell us the sun has entered a cycle of powerful flares and eruptions. They are catapulting to earth high-energy particles capable of wreaking havoc on electronic and communication systems that support our high-tech civilization. The result may be damaged transformers, orbiting satellites, global positioning systems.

While not catastrophic, temporary computer glitches are commonplace. We have all been inconvenienced in banks, medical offices, and stores when clerks mournfully stare at blank screens and then at us, mumbling, "The network is down." Temporary outages are one thing, satellite crashes another. The tangible may not be as relevant as the cloud, but as necessary.

Over time I grew more comfortable with roads I wouldn't have chosen earlier in life. Change is inevitable. I began to see my goal of "traditional, warm, comfortable" in a new light. White wasn't always cold. Traditional is not always desirable. Comfortable might be stagnation.

Arts and crafts I undertook at the outset helped me navigate a tangible road. Willa Cather's heroine started down a well-worn path. At the curve in the road she saw her life in new ways. Turns out I was more like the girl in the Jules Breton painting she wrote about than I imagined.

What is extraneous and what is essential changes depending on what kind of box we are in. Voltaire knew that.

Now I know too.

"Place on one side of the scales the actual advantages of the most sublime sciences, and on the other side the advantages of the mechanical arts... You will discover that far more praise has been heaped upon those men who spend their time making us believe we are happy, than on those who actually bring us happiness. How strangely we judge!"
—Denis Diderot, 1713-1784

MORE THAN MEETS THE EYE

Sometimes a simple idea isn't simple. Or perhaps it is that while an idea may be simple, its execution is not.

Take bookbinding for example. Books are common enough. Paperbacks have been flourishing since 1931 when Albatross Books began publishing them en masse. Many are inexpensive. People leave them behind in hotels, subway cars, waiting rooms. They are part of the ordinary flotsam and jetsam of living. I love reading books. In a burst of enthusiasm during what I call my "pioneer phase" I decided to learn to make my own. How hard could it be?

The oldest non-profit community center for arts in the Northwest, Maude Kerns Art Center was located in a converted church near the University of Oregon. Named for the teacher of generations of art teachers, Kerns was famous for three things: realistic landscapes, abstract exploration of color and form, and incorporating music in her teaching. Reading the Center bulletin, I winced, remembering my ill-fated childhood experience with music and art. But the mission statement was heartening: "To nurture artistic expression and creativity in the individual and cultivate an understanding of art and culture in the community." There were hundreds of choices. I picked bookbinding.

The tools spread out on the table at the front of the class were the first clue I was unprepared. Some I recognized—knives, needles, mallets, chisels, C-clamps. Many more were a mystery. Looking at them I felt I had wandered into Mary Shelley's "Frankenstein." Later they had names: band nippers, awls, pressing irons, bone folders, and a little brass shell attached to a wooden handle called a fillet. Binders use it to make straight lines on leather.

I imagined making books as folding paper in half and securing it somehow (glue perhaps?) with a cover, which bookbinders call "boards". I didn't consider there are different kinds of paper or cardboard or even adhesives.

My idea wasn't far off…if I had been living in the fifth century when that was more or less the process. Accordion folded scrolls were flattened, then turned into books with sheets tied together at one side through holes punched in the margin.

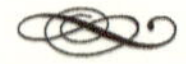

The teacher began by holding up a newsprint piece 12 by 18 inches. She folded and refolded it into ten possible shapes for a book. Her point: size and proportion matter. What you are doing depends on why you are doing it.

My journey with book making was memorable, not for the dozen or so small books I made with heavy papers and fabric covers in vintage nineteenth century prints, but for the lessons I learned about the folly of underestimating the ordinary.

There were other lessons. One took years to sink in. There is a gap between the world of the abstract and the world of the practical. It is an old division. At the heart of Plato's *Republic* lies the idea that the highest form of reality resides not in "works and days" but in an ideal realism of "essences." I spent hours trying to convey his concepts to high school and college students—always with mixed success. Most high school students were shrewd enough to placate me by agreeing that the idea of an apple (or a bed, which Plato had used as an example) was more substantial than the apple or bed itself. Exhausted college students were less receptive. They would groan and roll their red-rimmed eyes.

The effect of this doctrine is to redirect our attention away from arts and crafts, the nuts and bolts of everyday life, to a higher sphere beyond the ravages of time. The place of honor belongs to the philosopher, who dwells entirely in the realm of Ideas.

The hierarchy of head over hand, mind over body, theory over practice, is deeply rooted in the classical age. Even Aristotle says, "But as more arts were invented, and some were directed to the necessities of life, others to recreation, the inventions of the latter were naturally always regarded as wiser than the inventions of the former, because their branches of knowledge did not aim at utility."

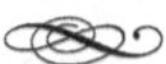

Laboring to construct a single book took weeks. Reading one took days. I saw why Plato saw the mechanical arts as debasing. In the fifth century B.C. the majority of the work—mechanical, industrial, agricultural—was performed by slaves. Work became associated with slavery. Only the free citizen had time to think.

But measuring and sewing the bindings of my simple books, I knew I was both working and thinking. Buried in the Greek language is a word, "poiesis." It is the same word—used to describe the work of both mechanic and poet. In modern times we are accustomed to thinking of the inspired artist and the disciplined worker as opposite human types who have nothing in common. But they are more alike than different. Despite what Greeks thought, their language didn't make any distinction between the work of artists or builders, architects or philosophers. A single word described their otherwise disconnected efforts. Different manifestations. One spirit. Poiesis became a cornerstone of my philosophy for teaching and for life—think and do. Either alone is insufficient.

On a high shelf in the back of a little used utility closet in my home is a large wooden box. In it are a glue gun, hooks, darning needles, wax paper, heavy cardboard, cloth scraps, and a small silver clamp. They are all that remain of my bookbinding years. Though I no longer make books, learning about their history, from the public libraries of Rome to the fifteenth century Byzantine emperors who paraded elaborate books on gold rods through the streets in public processions, made me appreciate them in new ways.

I keep the box to remind me about the craft of bookbinding. Paper books are disappearing. But the form of the book itself is part of the meaning. If we forget the form—small thin volumes, large extravagant tabletop glossies, earnest textbooks, soft cover graphic collections; the smooth feel of pages ruffling whispers as they turn, we lose something of ourselves.

"What is pronounced strengthens itself," the Polish poet Czeslaw Milosz wrote. "What is not pronounced leads to non-existence." When my mother-in-law died at 101, she had among her papers the book I made for her three decades before. On the flyleaf I wrote, "To Grandma Koch with love. I hope you will write some of your memories here for us to keep."

She kept the book, with its tiny brown and yellow fabric cover, on her dresser. It is on my dresser now. When I look at it I can hear her voice, telling tales of her childhood—a childhood that began in 1910. Long ago. Close at hand.

Bookbinding taught me ordinary things aren't ordinary. They contain yesterday's skills, talents, and sometimes, today's stories.

Tomorrow they will be our memories.

In from the Cold

*T*he unassuming white clapboard house on a busy street had a small sign over the door—"Painting Classes and Supplies." Below it a cheerful banner whipped in the dreary northwest rain. "Free Demonstration Today" wiggled back and forth in the wind. Leaving the gloomy wet behind I stepped across the threshold into a world as colorful as the one Dorothy found in Oz. Nothing was ever quite the same again.

The presenter, a chatty dark haired woman, looked more like a suburban hostess than the forest ranger's wife she was—a person who began decorative painting during ten years of remote Alaskan tours. Oregon wasn't Alaska, but I could identify. I too felt isolated and lost in a new place with not a clue how to decorate a home or much money to spend on the process. Loneliness doesn't depend on geography.

Her voice rose and fell as she talked about the American craft movement and swiped color on the wood and metal objects around her at the same time. William Morris, inventor of the Morris chair and founder of England's nineteenth century movement, had inspired Americans of modest means to take the decoration of their homes and furniture into their own hands. By the end of her demonstration her paintbrush coaxed several simple objects—a ladle, a wooden shoe, and an oven rack pull—into a life beyond functionality. It was like watching the mice transform Cinderella's drab second-hand dress into something that was still a dress, but a prettier one.

I wondered if it could do the same for me. Could I be more than a caregiver, housekeeper, cook, gardener— important jobs, functional jobs, exhausting in their relentlessness? Jackson Pollock characterized art as an act of "self-discovery," positioning the experience of the individual—not the work—at the center of the endeavor. I didn't need to be the center of anything. I needed something else. Tole painting became that something. It helped me develop an undiscovered corner of my life... a corner where there were fewer obligations and more uninterrupted hours. A creative place. A quiet place.

Elizabeth von Trapp, granddaughter of Maria and Baron von Trapp, says about her own musical career, "Music has given me a place to be." I felt the same about my plunge into decorative arts. They weren't so much a "place to be" as "another place to be."

I took evening classes up and down the Willamette Valley— anywhere traveling teachers were demonstrating new techniques or interesting projects. Over time I painted butter churns, ornate plaques, wooden shutters, lap desks, clock faces, jewelry boxes, towel racks, metal pitchers, ladles. I would eye any stationary object and wonder if it would look better painted. Our once-empty house morphed into a vista of cluttered walls and crowded counters—testimony to my enthusiasm, if not skill. I joined generations of ordinary people who found ways to brighten their prosaic days with colors and patterns sprinkled amid life's daily routines.

Ten years later Oregon became part of our past. I kept a dozen or so wooden tole projects. Beyond the designs—cherries, gooseberries, pears, grapes, ornate Scandinavian florals—was a less obvious lesson I learned from preparing the wood. The more time I spent on the unglamorous, dirty work—stripping, sanding, staining, sealing—the better the finished piece. Shortcuts never worked. The paint flaked, the wood grain interfered, the brushes lost their shape whenever

I rushed. Today, a lifetime later, when the speed and demands of contemporary living make it easier, faster, and cheaper to buy things rather than make them I often wonder: What are the hidden costs of our shortcuts?

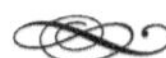

In the preface to *Collected Poems* Robert Frost wrote that a poem

...begins in delight and ends in wisdom. It inclines to the impulse, it assumes direction with the first line laid down, it runs a course of lucky events, and ends in a clarification of life—not necessarily a great clarification, such as sects and cults are founded on, but in a momentary stay against confusion.

Folk art painting works the same.

In the loneliness of a new place, terrified at the responsibilities of parenting, uncertain of the path, painting became an anchor to the past, a marker for the present, an unspoken wish for home.

Life unfolded. There were other cities, other homes, other lives to live. When I returned to teaching high school my paint box was relegated to the garage. Every fall I rummaged through it to find a worn piece of sandpaper to tack on the classroom bulletin board. It was a reminder from my painting days…take time.

It pays off. In painting. In teaching. In life.

New Directions

Eager for a new surface to paint on, I enrolled in a glass-painting seminar. Its use in decoration has a long history dating to early Egyptian culture. By the tenth century it had become part of medieval architecture. Courting mirrors with decorated glass panels were among the prized exports when trade with China was flourishing. The techniques are complicated. The results are beautiful.

The seminar subject was dimensional violets on five small panes of window glass. Part of the lush bouquet was painted on each slab. The objective was to teach depth and perspective by having us mix our own shades of blue and purple, then combine the design with colors that magnified depth.

Some of us added crimson to get brighter violets. Others added raw umber to create almost black purple. I mixed blue and purple equally to create a third shade. My project was conventional, careful, and complete—until I looked at some of my classmates' efforts. Students who ignored the directions did the most arresting designs. Mixing different colors altogether and deconstructing their bouquets, they had stems and outlandish flowers wandering away from the primary design in clever alternative patterns. When the glass was stacked they had created unique provocative arrangements using

16

their imaginations. I accomplished what the teacher expected. Yet rather than satisfied, I was disappointed. It was some years before I understood why.

Not long age New York's American Folk Art Museum was considering dissolving itself and dispersing its art to the Smithsonian. At the last moment its trustees and the Ford Foundation rescued it. New York's Cultural Affairs Commissioner said, "This is a wonderful outcome. People are increasingly recognizing the value and the excitement of folk art, outsider art."

That's good news. Being able to look back is important, but not enough. Old art, whether magnificent or mundane, is always the raw material of new art. The artist's job is to build on it or transform it, not offer up comforting familiarity as a talisman against the void. That was the problem with my glass project.

It was a bridge backward. Much later, painting became a path forward. The eclectic, defiant, thought-provoking, appealing violet creations I admired grew from being able to see something that wasn't there before. Some of us took a simple design from "outsider art" and made it new. I did not. My flowers were pretty, predictable, and pedestrian. But I learned. I spent a year working with dimensional designs. Every project grew more interesting, more playful, more original. I began to understand what I could do if I looked beyond the obvious.

The violets are gone now, broken in one of our household relocations. Their lesson remains. New endings can come from conventional beginnings by using old tools in different ways.

The only energy it takes is the courage to use our imagination. It's the energy we need in a world where the road has grown rockier and our declining standard of living is called "the new normal."

Stacking the glass in a different order. It's a good idea. It may fail, but we won't know unless we try.

One January years later I scanned my new spring term last period class list, fearing the rumor I heard in the faculty room was true. It was. One of the most disruptive high school seniors was in my elective "The Short Story." He made his first appearance by swinging into the room off the doorjamb like Tarzan dropping from a tree. Six feet four inches of uncontrolled energy, he electrified the all-boy class with his defiance, his arrogance, his slick BMW in the student parking lot, and his athletic scholarship to the University of San Diego if he passed every class the last term.

The first week was a nightmare. Thirty teenage boys after lunch. I was trapped in a movie—"'Ferris Bueller's Day Off'-meets-'Lord of the Flies.'" The ringleader senior spent most of his time squirming in desks too small, sending paper airplanes soaring, sabotaging class discussions, sauntering around the classroom at will.

Weeks dragged by. Each worse than before. Early one Monday I was standing on the large shag entry rug at home, calling last instructions to my own children before we headed separate ways. Looking down at the blue and white pattern, I got an idea. I dragged the rug to the car and headed to work. Not the least of my nemesis's problems was he was uncomfortable in the school furniture.

Sixth period arrived. I suggested if someone was too tired, too distracted, or too stressed to sit in a desk they could sit on the rug… as long as they tracked with the class. It had worked when I was a preschool teacher—why not try it with high school seniors? Many of them act like overgrown preschoolers themselves. There's even a name for their behavior—"the Peter Pan principle." Like Peter, growing up is something to be avoided. Many adults they know don't look like they're having much fun. No point in rushing the future, they think.

The rug was a curiosity. Most students thought it was uncool. The troublemaker did not. He stretched out like a resting lion. The effect on the class was stunning. Everyone was calmer.

The final project was to write a short story. He wrote about a magic carpet that took a boy to a place where people didn't have so many rules or expectations. At the end he added a note—"Your class wasn't so bad after all. Thanks. I'd like to get you a present."

I suggested violets.

Eccentric Circles

In spring of 1926 writer Sherwood Anderson wrote to his seventeen-year-old son, John, who was contemplating his future, "

> If I had my own life to lead over I presume I would still be a writer but I am sure I would give my first attention to learning how to do things directly with my hands. Nothing gives quite the satisfaction that doing things brings.

There was a time I thought education was defined by majors and minors. Classes set down a map that would guide the rest of my life. "Doing" equated "school." For someone like me, raised in a military family and often uprooted, school was both the answer to the future and a bastion against being the outsider in the present. I might not know anyone, but at least I understood public school. Books were the same everywhere. Heavy, shabby at the edges, official stamps on the inside cover above the names of the previous "owners." Textbooks made me part of an invisible club.

It was no surprise I paid no attention to running a household or creating a home. In the subtle ways past generations shape future ones, Mother survived a childhood of drudgery compounded by poverty and parents with grade school educations. She wanted neither for her children. She ran the house. I studied. My much younger sister played. When faced with a home of my own, the shock was electric. I had no idea what to do.

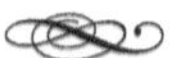

If school didn't prepare me for household life, it did leave me with something—the discipline to structure my time toward a goal. Turning empty rooms into welcoming spaces was my first focus. In a dozen homes through my adult life there have been plenty of spaces to fill.

Aristotle said that all people by nature desire to know. I wanted to learn everything about homemaking. I hooked rugs using a latch hook hinge. Pulling the yarn through stiff burlap and knotting the back I was "channeling" a craft that hadn't been popular in America for two hundred years. I didn't care.

Originally made from scraps left in English weaving mills, hooked rugs were part of what wealthy women called "the thumb craft of poverty." After 1830 rich people preferred machine made floor coverings. I could hook and watch children at the same time. Both grew. It was easier to measure the progress of the rugs.

The designs captured feelings I wanted around my fledging family. One large beige and brown landscape, with a burnt orange sun sinking at the horizon, was the view from our New Mexico apartment every evening. In art horizontal directions are quiet, calm, restful. The rug was a wish.

No sooner would one rug be completed than I would plunge into another. Starting and finishing imposed a frame on time, something I missed after years of school bells. In a later project there was a birch grove in the snow, a yellow moon rising behind slashing diagonal branches and vertical trunks. Diagonals create movement, verticals stability and strength. The rug was a prayer.

Still later there were stenciled canvas floor cloths with repeating fruit and flower motifs bordering colorful center patterns. Those too had fallen out of style, replaced by linoleum at the end of the nineteenth century. The house was a kind of history laboratory. No part was exempt. There were countless sets of cross-stitch pillowcases, tiny dough flower arrangements, unfortunate pipe cleaner turkey centerpieces, gaudy Christmas stockings, Ball mason candle holders, corn husk dolls and holiday ornaments.

For two or three messy years there were macramé curtains and wall hangings, plant holders, even intricate necklaces—all in various states of knotting, strung everywhere. The dining room table disappeared beneath piles of cotton, hemp, yarn and beads. The projects were all descendants of thirteenth century Arab weavers. The techniques had made their way to England in the 1600s. I started large window coverings on wooden dowels. Dozens of cords snaked across the room. It was a process rather like doing an old fashioned Maypole dance by yourself. The craft hadn't been popular since the Victorian era, when *Sylvia's Book of Macramé Lace* topped the bestseller list in 1882. I was undeterred.

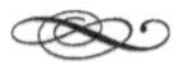

It was humbling to glimpse how hard earlier generations worked, not only in factories and on farms, but also in their domestic pursuits. I began to understand the pattern of my work as a set of eccentric circles. In geometry they are circles nested inside one another, where one contains the center of them all. The projects were many. The shared center was making a home…literally.

In the introduction to Bill Bryson's history of private life, *At Home*, he says,

> …whatever happens in the world—whatever is discovered or created or bitterly fought over—eventually ends up, in one way or another, in your house. Wars, famines, the Industrial Revolution, the Enlightenment—they are all there in your sofas and chests of drawers, tucked in the folds of your cur-

tains…in the paint on your walls. Houses are refuges from history. They are where history ends up.

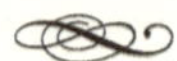

The children grew. I returned to what society called "work"; that is, work outside the household. It is a peculiar distinction, suggesting life at home isn't work. In both places activities are sometimes creative, often mundane. Both have their share of boredom and stress. But only one has a salary. For many years I apologized for the time I spent at home. I no longer do. It's the old Gatsby spin: the light through the windows is always more enchanting when viewed from the street outside.

In art making one line longer and wider than the rest will create a dominance of direction, which unifies a painting. The dominant line unifying my life grew wider because of my years at home—something I didn't expect. I benefited from my formal education—the rigors of classwork, the discipline of study, but I learned equally valuable lessons from the process of creating a place for family. Walking though my house today it has become a home. Not because of the things I made. Because of the memories attached to them.

In the spring of life I practiced arts and crafts of earlier generations. It is autumn now. Thomas Wolfe was right when he wrote:

All things on earth point home in old October; Sailors to sea, travelers to wall and fences, hunters to field and hollow and the long voice of the hounds, the lover to the love he has forsaken.

Careers end. Memories fade. Homes last.
In our hearts."

Found and Lost

The smooth, suave agent repeated
what he had been saying all week.
"California prices are difficult."

Sixty houses later, shirt wrinkled,
tie loose, glossy flyers filling
his luxury car, through clenched teeth he snapped,
"This is the last one in your range."

The stucco house squatted amid
a broken drip system. Anemic
plants gasped. Sunlight crept
through holes in the garage roof.
Transmission wires loomed in back.
The view in front—a fence.

Past the weedy rock river bed we
stepped into the gloom through
imitation raised panel double doors
better suited for a cheap motel.

The realtor's disembodied voice
drifted across the shadows.
"The family room windows
are filled in to block the house next door."

Peering into the dark we said,
"We'll take it."

Across the room we heard a thud
as the multiple listing book hit the floor.

Another thump followed. The
sound of a door closing in
our hearts.

Time to begin. Again.

Part Two

ETCHES IN TIME

"I'll call for pen and ink, and write my mind."
—Shakespeare, "Henry VI, Part I"

Looking for Perfect

We are a restive species, driven by some natural tendency to want to outdo ourselves. It is an expression of the universal tendency Darwin described when he wrote, "As natural selection works solely by and for the good of each being, all corporeal and mental environments will tend toward perfection."

Or maybe it is, as French philosopher J.B. Robinet suggested, a tendency unique to human minds, whose "destiny can be nothing other than to exercise imagination, to invent, and to perfect."

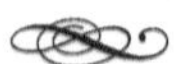

In either case the goal is unattainable. Perfect is like a vanishing point in painting—an imaginary point at infinity toward which every major course is directed. In math it is called an asymptotic limit: an ideal that is approachable yet never realizable.

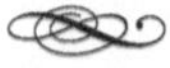

In the twentieth century handwriting was another place where perfection seemed important, in part because people thought one's character could be improved by working on one's handwriting. Alfred Binet, who came up with the Stanford-Binet IQ test, believed there

26

was a "science of graphology" that revealed a person's character in their handwriting. It is an idea still popular in Europe.

My third grade teacher, Mrs. Taltavall, was a devotee. She took our penmanship lessons as seriously as she did every other content area. A large, florid woman, she stood in front of the class at the appointed time every day, like a dance master before a ballet lesson. She would sway back and forth, arms shooting up or dropping down like an airport ground-crew worker guiding a plane to its gate, as we followed her body language with our pencils. I liked the symmetry and challenge of getting the shapes "just right"…though "just right" never happened.

What did happen was more modest but far reaching: I developed a love for the process and for the tools…fat pencils, thin pencils, and later the fountain pens with their clever levers for loading ink. My girlfriends and I experimented…heart-dotted i's, switching slants, adding self-conscious swirls and hooks. Mrs. Taltavall tolerated all but the last. Clutching her weathered copy of Milton Bunker's 1939 book *What Handwriting Tells You About Yourself, Your Friends, and Famous People*, she warned that hooks betrayed an acquisitive and manipulative character.

It followed for us that we could improve our character by improving our handwriting. It was a residue from the nineteenth century golden age of penmanship. In the 1800s Platt Rogers Spencer lacked the money to buy paper but his passion for handwriting was so great he practiced on leaves and bark, in the snow, and on the sandy beaches of Lake Erie where his sometimes obsessive script would stretch for half a mile. People who followed him believed "they learned to train the mind by disciplining the hand." Spenserian writing is gone now, living on mostly in the Coca Cola Company logo. Once it was the official style of government clerks and upper-class citizens.

Years later I began to admire artist Thomas Eakins. He is best known for his paintings of taut rowers on the Schuylkill River in Philadelphia. What is less known about him is that his father was a master penman who would put the whole family to work during diploma season. Thomas was his protégé, and his lessons in script influenced his orderly approach to art.

It has influenced me too. Good handwriting is one of those civilizing achievements, like dressing or cooking well, that takes the work of necessity and saves it from becoming mundane. It may not reveal intelligence or personality type, but it does speak to an effort to be understood.

The cover of the *Christian Science Monitor* on September 19, 2011 proclaimed, "How Apple won over the world…It understood the power of being itself."

Inside, one former employee says,

> Apple has always been on a journey to be its best self…and enable their customers to be their best self too. Its greatest strength is its obsessiveness about everything. From how the stores are laid out, to design, packaging, the symmetry of their mother board, their goal is perfection.

Penmanship and painting taught me perfection isn't attainable. Penmanship class showed me practice counts. In painting I learned vanishing points help organize space and depth, what is important and what needs to recede.

Practice. Organize. Soften. We have more choices than we imagine.

Soul Shaping

One Christmas Jim brought home a set of calligraphy pens, the least wanted item in his office holiday party swap gift exchange. A beheaded fountain pen and collection of odd-looking nibs, they were left behind by the disappointed recipient. I was delighted. It was like meeting an old friend after a long absence. I owned a set myself, now long lost, for an Oregon printing class many years before.

The invention of writing, which Carlyle called "the most miraculous of all things man has devised," made possible the beginning of the book. It was natural after I learned how books were made to venture on to what was inside them. The first true written language appeared about 3000 B.C., when ancient Sumerians developed cuneiform—a series of wedge-shaped letters that, besides preserving records, also created a beautiful all-over decorative design. It was as much art as information storage. The history, the patterns, the techniques attracted me.

The modern world is hard to recognize. Although in the current age of Google and AmazonPrime nearly everything ever written can be accessed within seconds or delivered within days, we still feel unsure and overwhelmed. At least I do. Facts are cheap and easy; the cell phone is an infinite library. Instead of making us more confident, we are becoming more tentative, or worse, more susceptible to quick solutions. As psychologist Herbert Simon wrote, "A wealth of information creates a poverty of attention."

Stay-at-home mothers are distracted at every turn, in every age. Calligraphy lessons became a perfect antidote to my interrupted daytime life. I enrolled in "Beginning Forms" at Eugene's Maude Kerns Art Center.

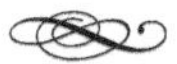

I discovered calligraphy as the Northwest was emerging as the west coast center of the long-dormant art. Governor Tom McCall named Lloyd Reynolds, founder of the Western Branch of the Society for Italic Handwriting and instructor at Reed College, Oregon's first "Calligrapher Laureate" in 1978 as I began my class.

Reynolds' influence was everywhere. His idea was calligraphy was always present in varying forms around us. Studying those forms would encourage a new awareness of the world.

I practiced in the pre-dawn morning hours before the children were awake. It became a time of focus and meditation as I twisted the broad-edged square cut pen to decorate note cards with sayings I found or had written. In the quiet at dawn I was not just lettering, but talking to myself. I sent collections on colored linen paper to my parents and in-laws. Most were questions. Among them:

"What if the rain never stopped? The earth would turn into one big sponge for wiping the universe clean."

"Who are teachers? The world is full of teachers, each of us for others and ourselves."

"What is soul? Perhaps it is a longing for an Infinite that is elusive in a finite world."

The careful writing helped me think. My answers might be different now but the process still works.

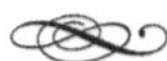

At about the same time I was learning calligraphy Steve Jobs, founder of Apple and arguably a man who changed the world, was at Reed—studying calligraphy. In his biography he said,

> I learned about serif and san serif typefaces, about varying the amount of space between different letter combinations, about what makes great typography great. It was beautiful, historical, artistically subtle in a way science can't capture, and I found it fascinating. None of it had any practical application. But ten years later when we were designing the first Mac it all came back to me. And we designed it all into the Mac.

Today I have access to hundreds of fonts on my pull-down menu. Thousands are available as phone apps. Even so I've begun practicing my letterforms again with the cast-off pen set. The discipline reminds me of the world cultures, myths, and even the architectural forms that make life layered and beautiful.

I think Steve Jobs would approve. It's the Apple motto: Think Different.

Moving On

Something was wrong. I couldn't put my finger on it. What could it be?

Most of my graduate students were Generation Ys…born after 1982, raised in a digital world. Slogging through various credentials and degree programs at the end of their long workdays made it difficult for them to focus. The cares and worries of their days came with them every week. Their commutes, their own course preparations and classroom management challenges, and their responsibilities at home hung around them like Marley's chains in Dickens' *Christmas Carol.* For any teacher, it's a problem. All students are difficult to focus, no matter what their age. I had decades of experience but it wasn't helping. Things weren't going well.

To counter the distracted hum and glazed looks I filled a large easel at the front of the room with "presenting questions" to jumpstart the evening. Written in careful cursive, I reasoned the sheets would become part of the class record and help them remember what we were doing. As weeks passed the room walls filled with topics from earlier sessions. It was like living inside a house with walls of grace-full, looping Palmer writing. It seemed like a good idea—sort of like "dinner special" easels in restaurant waiting areas. It wasn't working.

Students rummaged in their backpacks, pulled out papers, laptops, books, talked to each other, or gazed at the clock, willing it to advance. The same few people opened every discussion. Midway through the term, a thirty-something middle school history teacher approached me as I was putting the finishing touches on my easel questions. Twisting his hands, he lowered his eyes. Gesturing at the sheet behind me I beamed, "Hi Mark. Would you like to add something?"

Shoulders hunched, he sighed. "Some of us can't read your handwriting." He rushed on, "We only print or keyboard. We didn't learn cursive."

I'm not sure which of us was more embarrassed. My cursive writing days at school screeched to a halt. It was 1999. I converted to block printing. Class discussions perked up. I took down the posters around the room, rolled them into a fat cylinder, and propped them behind my office door. I was the only one who missed them.

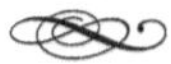

Cursive writing has become a quaint historical artifact, joining milkmen, land line telephones, newspaper delivery boys, even newspapers themselves. Schools devote little, if any, time to it. Many states no longer mention it in their curriculum standards. In spring, 2011, the Indiana State Department of Education sent a letter to all its families—beginning the next fall public schools would no longer teach cursive writing. However, students would be expected to be proficient in keyboarding.

Three arguments are carrying the day: everyone works and plays on keyboards now; standardized test preparation takes too much time to "give up" precious minutes to handwriting; and schools reflect a society which now believes writing is both difficult and pointless.

Difficult? Maybe. Pointless? No.

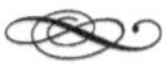

I can still see my grade school blank newsprint books with their mottled black covers. Fifty empty pages, with alternating solid and dotted blue lines like freeway lane markers, filled with my daily handwriting efforts. The books stacked up in our storage cubbies, testimony to our "progress." Penmanship lessons were different—a change from the rest of the curriculum. The loops and tails, chubby circles, flourishes, slants that made whole lines look like Radio City Music Hall dancers doing high kicks, were a tangible link between what I was thinking and what I was doing. Half a century later holding a pencil above blank paper I still feel my brain shifting…lining up like a golfer before a putt.

The imperceptible hum of the computer with its musical greeting and blue screen evokes a different response—more detached, more mechanical. For me, the pencil is more intimate than the keyboard. When ideas are fragile and just taking shape my brain and my heart don't want to be distracted by a screen. Afterwards, the clever computer makes shaping easier. But there needs to be something to shape. Every important paper, letter, project—including my dissertation— began with a pencil. They still do.

Learning from students is one of the great gifts of teaching. It's also a survival technique. James Russell Lowe was right. He observed, "New occasions teach new duties." I bought colored markers and devised a kind of print and icon system they understood immediately. Without the cursive posters hanging around, they began to create their own discussion questions. To me the new easel sheet markings looked like drunken footprints staggering across a sandy white beach. The students, on the other hand, saw them as information they could access at a glance.

I miss cursive writing. But when I find myself getting maudlin about its virtues I remember my favorite Melville story, "Bartleby the Scrivener—A Story of Wall Street." In it, the complexities of the bond between individuals and society unfold in a law office where Bartleby spends his day copying documents. The lawyer narrator says:

> At first Bartleby did an extraordinary quantity of writing. As if long famishing for something to copy, he seemed to gorge himself on my documents. There was no pause for digestion. He ran a day and night line, copying by sunlight and candlelight. I should have been quite delighted with his application, had he been cheerfully industrious. But he wrote on silently, politely, mechanically.
>
> It is of course an indispensable part of a scrivener's business to verify the accuracy of his copy, word by word. When there are two or more scriveners in an office, they assist each other in this examination, one reading from the copy, the other holding the original.
>
> It is a very dull, wearisome and lethargic affair. I can readily imagine that, for some sanguine temperaments, it would be altogether intolerable.
>
> For example, I cannot credit that the mettlesome poet, Byron, would have contentedly sat down with Bartleby to examine a law document of, say five hundred pages, closely written in a crimpy hand.

Finally Bartleby rebels, responding to every request to copy or check his writing with the famous words (for every student who reads the story), "I prefer not to."

The narrator's world is forever changed as he tries to understand this assault on the conventional order. In the same way, the end of cursive is a reflection of a changing society…a society in the throes of what historians William Strauss and Neil Howe call "The Unraveling." It is a recurring generational pattern that will result in a redefinition of how we work, live, play, pray, communicate.

Bartleby's defiance helps the lawyer redefine his world. It expands beyond his workplace walls to include a man who wants to be acknowledged for other than his ability to copy documents.

For my students' cursive writing was a barrier—for Bartleby, a prison separating him from life beyond work—for me, a catalyst for thinking. Even more, the repetition of those childhood drills led to pride in something created by hand…built on bedrock of time-consuming labor. Practice had other benefits too. One was the lesson that success depends more on perseverance than speed. The computer works at lightening pace. My students turned out papers in record time. But reading them, and later reading disjointed graduate papers in other schools, I think of Samuel Johnson, who once said in a different context, "What is written without effort is in general read without pleasure."

Coherent arguments need structure. So do engaging paintings. In art, selective repetition adds unity to compositions. Cursive writing was good practice for both. I am glad I have a computer—sleek, fast, a universe of information at my fingertips. It does almost everything, as does its newer next-generation competition: convenient handheld devices destined to replace desktops.

Almost everything. The idea seeds for essays, or paintings, or letters to friends—don't happen on the screen. They begin somewhere more mysterious, more idiosyncratic, more intimate. They begin in the subconscious, percolating up, emerging half-formed, needing polish. Technology is good for polish.

New ages use different tools for problem solving, for creating, for communicating. Pencils belong to yesterday. DaVinci sketched with a pencil. Steinbeck and Hemingway wrote their manuscripts with them. Thoreau manufactured some of the best in New England himself. Edison always kept one in his pocket.

I've got a stubby pencil in my pocket, too. The eraser is worn down. When I am stuck on a thorny problem I doodle handwriting shapes in the margins of my tablet or on scraps of paper. It helps every time.

As chief operating officer at Facebook, Silicon Valley power broker Sheryl Sandberg is Number Two in command at the world's largest social network. Every day she brings to work a Windows laptop computer, an Apple iPad, Android and Blackberry phones. "I try everything," she says. "I have over 3000 friends to communicate with. My CEO, Mark Zuckerberg, prefers instant-message chat. My sister calls on a cell phone. My husband prefers e-mail."

Students who compose on keyboards tell me when they are stuck they switch screens, check their email or Facebook page, text a friend, or spend time playing games.

The time may come when contemporary connections become as suffocating for modern life as Bartleby's law office existence. Meanwhile, I'll sharpen my pencil. Someone may need to borrow it if there is a power outage.

There will be.

*"...and be it further enacted that, to facilitate the transportation of
letters by mail, the Postmaster General be authorized to prepare
postage stamps which when attached to any letter or packet, shall
be evidence of prepayment of the postage chargeable on such letter."*
—Act of Congress, March 3, 1847

The World Comes Home

On August 18, 2011, National Public Radio ran another in
a long line of news stories on the fate of the postal service.
Awash in debt, use declining, the conventional view is its demise
is inevitable. The NPR story, "There's Always Work at the Post
Office," focused on some of the 120,000 jobs being cut in the
current round of lay-offs. The human toll is steep. The interviews
were poignant. The despair seeped through the radio into the
room. However sad the losses, I listened for things I didn't hear.

Once employing over 790,000 workers, proponents and detractors
alike scoff at the antiquated idea of delivering paper mail anywhere
in the country to anyone, rich or poor, for under fifty cents. "That's
the point!" I want to shout. All of us—found, and treated equally, no
matter what our circumstances. Every letter brings the ghost of the
venerable old institution's founder, Benjamin Franklin. He knew when
he began in 1775 it was a kind of glue for our fragile experiment in
self-government. Riding horseback through the early colonies drum-
ming up support for his idea, he saw the postal service as a way to carry
his message: "Where liberty dwells, there is my country."

Our country isn't new anymore, but it is still fragile. We have less
in common. But we still share the mail…every town, every village,

every city. It's a way to orient the traveler, the wanderer, the seeker, the resident. There's friendliness in a mailbox. Letters from wealthy people snuggle next to those from struggling students; rural farmers send news jammed next to serial tech entrepreneurs recounting their good fortune. Ph.D.s and children are there, all together, treated the same. Postmarks are far-flung. But every piece shares one similarity—the small notation stamped in the corner—U.S. Postage. It's glue.

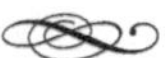

Growing up in a military family means growing up on the move. One of my childhood chores was getting the mail for Mother. At the end of snowy New England driveways, or in precarious metal containers outside California bungalows, or in apartment lobby wall boxes with tiny keys, I would find mail. The mailman fascinated me—what he brought, how he found us. His blue uniform and enormous leather satchel made every city feel like home.

Mother would give me the discarded envelopes. I delivered them to my dolls. When I tired of the game I would cut the stamps off and save them. Most were purple three-cent denominations. A few were red airplane images. They were more important—six cents. We moved again and again. The stamps moved with me in an old shoebox. They reminded me of homes left behind. It was another kind of glue.

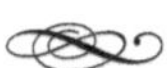

1971 arrived. I was an expectant mother in a small second floor apartment behind a gas station in Eugene, Oregon. Our first purchase was a huge desk with a laminated wood top and chrome legs. In front of it we squeezed a secondhand blond crib, adorned with the teeth marks of its four previous occupants. We figured we didn't need much else. After all, I first slept in a dresser drawer so this was an upgrade. On July 20, 1971, I wrote in my journal:

Summer is upon us…interminable. The world reflects my own restlessness—what will become of me now that I have set aside one career, well defined, for another, not defined at all? Am I strong enough to be curious, eager for each day—without a pre-designated series of challenges? I dream of writing, but wonder how much I have to say. I dream of art projects—warm, friendly things, and wonder if my imagination can take me there. The change from daughter to mother—what a giant step! Is my stride long enough?

Unpacking, I discovered my old stamp-filled shoebox. Sifting through the tiny reminders of time gone by, an idea dawned on me. I might be lost, but the mail would find me. I began to collect postage stamps in earnest. They are beautiful. They tell stories. Former Postmaster General Arthur Summerfield said of them, "The postage stamps of a nation are a picture gallery of its glories. They depict in miniature its famous men and women, the great events of its history, its organizations, its industries, its natural wonders." I joined the Postal Commemorative Society, which delivered first day issue stamps from their point of origin to me for twenty-five years. No matter where we lived, they found their way…home.

People who have garages use them for many things—the least of which is their cars. Ours has a long wall of cupboards lined with rows and rows of binders—filled with a lifetime stamp collection. They tell their own stories, and help mark the passage of our lives. Looking at the cupboard one day, 1998 caught my eye. Stamps were thirty-two cents that year. Among those featured was the US Postal Service's Classic Collection of twenty masterpieces of American art over four centuries.

The artists were from many parts of the country. A few were born abroad. Some were professionally trained—others self-taught. Their subjects ranged from Winslow Homer's landscapes to Mary Cassatt and Grant Wood's images of stoicism and self-reliance. 1998 was a hard year. My job had become untenable. One son struggled with health issues. The other with a shaky business start-up. The little stamps arrived like Lilliputian emissaries—bringing pictures that reminded me life is a very long story. Every age had challenges. Every age met them. We could too.

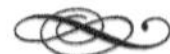

One can purchase postage stamps now with "Forever" as the monetary value. If people buy them at all it is a hedge against price increases they know are coming. I don't. Nor do I buy them online or at the various places that sell stamps—grocery stores, drug stores, convenience stores, box stores. I go to the Post Office, stand in line surrounded by people sending bulky packages or renewing their passports. I think of the sturdy gray building, flag flying overhead, as a way station for travelers. I like imagining where their packages are going. Where their passports will take them.

A tiny birdlike clerk with dyed jet-black hair motions people forward. She has worked in the same spot for twenty-six years. I study the current first class options, choose a half dozen sheets or so each visit, and bring them home in a large wax paper envelope. Nothing lasts forever. This ritual is on borrowed time. For most people it is aggravating to stand in lines…at least at the Post Office. Frivolous to buy stamps. Foolish to care about mail. Fossil-like to use it.

Perhaps. Perhaps not. Stamps made my world bigger. They inspired me. They helped me create a home in my heart for wonders I might have otherwise overlooked.

It's easy to focus on the negative…in politics, in neighborhoods, in general. Stamps highlight the astonishing beauty and courage of our human story. Like summer days that seem more special as they end, I will miss them when they're gone.

Maya Angelou said, "I long, as does every human being, to be at home wherever I find myself."

When stamps found me, I knew I was there.

REDISCOVERY

At age ninety-three Pablo Casals wrote,

For the past eighty years I have started each day in the same manner. I go to the piano, and I play two preludes and fugues of Bach. It is sort of a benediction on the house, but that's not its only meaning. It is a rediscovery of the world in which I have the joy of being a part.

Morning routines. We all have them though parts change with age. Life with very small children creates one rhythm, teenagers another. Even with no one else to manage launching the day requires a certain presence of mind. Jim begins each morning as he has for many years—breakfast followed by a spiritual reading and meditation.

I begin by writing one letter…sometimes more. It is a habit I began as a young teacher. Hundreds of students passed through my classroom each year. Part of the fun was connecting with them, not just as students, but as people with lives filled with the joy and heartbreak that follow youth like twin shadows.

The end of a term or school year always brought a sense of loss as the community changed. Students moved on. So did teachers. It has been a recurring theme in my life. Always saying goodbye. People gone, like a turned kaleidoscope, but not forgotten.

I began writing letters to not just former students, but to people who had moved in and out of my life. I wrote to encourage, to congratulate, to share, to remember, to continue conversations. I still do. Sometimes in the morning quiet I open my address book at random and point. The names all remind me how lucky I have been in my encounter with the world. The letters are a kind of meditation.

Ereline McCord is an example. A dozen years ago my sister and I began accompanying our father to his family reunions in Green City, Missouri, a tiny town (population 683) he left in 1939. The narrow road from Kansas City winds through Hamilton, the birthplace of retailer J. C. Penney. On a whim we stopped at the Penney Mall, which is not a mall but a small building housing "Antiques, Collectibles, and Vintage," according to the faded sign out front. Everything in northern Missouri is in decline, including Hamilton.

At the counter was a cheerful man in overalls and a plaid shirt. Not the owner, he said, but married to her. Since we were the only customers he visited with us while we shopped. A former science and math teacher, he retired to his farm while his wife ran the shop.

"I'm just filling in today," he said. "My wife's under the weather a bit."

Charmed by him and saddened by the decay creeping through the heartland, I wrote them both a thank-you note afterwards. A thank you for taking time to visit with strangers, for their neat-as-a-pin shop, for their stories. Since that first encounter Mr. McCord has suffered two heart attacks. His wife reports he doesn't come into town very often, but she is still minding the store.

Every year we stop. She takes our picture. We catch up. We find something to buy. She adds the purchases by hand, rechecks her work, and opens an enormous ornate brass cash register to complete the transactions. She belongs to another age. Several times a year I post a letter to the address on her business card: "Penney Mall, Downtown Davis Street, Hamilton, Missouri 64644." It is a chance to catch up on a town time forgot, and to remember the people who live there.

Evening is here for postal service. My adult children tell me my correspondence is almost the only first-class mail they receive. The delivery is so inconsequential one of them forgets his mailbox for days at a time. "There's nothing but junk," he shrugs.

The new communication landscape is electronic—characterized by speed rather than reflection. Often it is cryptic—144 characters. Sometimes speed matters. Sometimes it doesn't.

I remember the old government highway safety slogan "Speed kills." In the early 1970s, as a result of the 1973 oil shock, the United States imposed new lower speed limits in an effort to save fuel. The first year road fatalities dropped by nine thousand people. But what wasn't taken into account was the cost of gas. Fewer people were driving. Speed can kill drivers. So can carelessness. Neglect. Inattention. The same can be said of relationships.

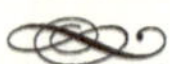

In my mid-twenties I worked a summer in Yellowstone National Park. Browsing one day in a second-hand store in Bozeman, Montana (while waiting for my laundry that was being beaten to death at the Laundromat next door), I discovered a special book. It is a letter collection by Sir Sydney Cockerell. In 1908 he became the director of the Fitzwilliam Museum in Cambridge, England. For the next three decades he spent much of his time thinking about paintings, sculpture, and prints. His ability to extract these objects from rich Englishmen became legendary. He transformed the Fitzwilliam into the distinguished institution it is now.

He lived in a time when friends communicated by letter. He corresponded with whole bunches of interesting people. Letters poured in. George Bernard Shaw used him as a confidant. So did T.H. White. There were people of all sorts—a Benedictine nun with whom he corresponded for forty-six years (each wrote the other about 750 letters); Walter Ivins, the keeper of prints at the Metropolitan Museum of Art; Katie Adams, a talented bookbinder. Many others.

The book, *The Best of Friends: Further Letters to Sydney Carlyle Cockerell*, contains hundreds of letters people wrote to him between 1900 and 1954 and a few of his replies. It's a reminder of what communication can be when it is laced with affection, intelligence, humor, and wisdom. Even the most mundane and instrumental among them had a civilized air, or at least a courteous one. More than anything else, it's the humanity of them that strikes me as so important.

Not long ago I read a question to an advice columnist in the local paper. A parent wanted to know if it was alright after a birthday party for children to send a general email message along the lines, "Thanks for coming to my party and for all the neat presents." The advisor suggested trying "to make it a little more specific" but allowed it was better than nothing. Really?

Letter writing is an art. Like other arts it connects people and leaves both the creator and receiver changed in some way. The letters I write, simple as they often are, are for me what playing Bach preludes were for Casals, or quiet meditation is for my husband. They celebrate the gift living is—the chance to create, to be, to do something with intention.

In the book *Joys and Sorrows* Casals says, "The music is never the same for me, never. Each day it is something new, fantastic, and unbelievable." Letter writing is like that. It is always new, always a privilege to think about others, always a chance to reconnect.

Though their topics are different, what I am saying at the core is "I miss seeing you. You are in my thoughts. You matter."

Life rediscovered. Every day.

Crossing the Border

For twenty years I have lived in a house with a laundry room—a big laundry room. Floor to ceiling cupboards wrap around three sides. A deep sink interrupts the tile counters that end where they meet the washer and dryer. Nevertheless, doing laundry there is a challenge. Stacks of greeting card supplies are everywhere—rubber stamps, ribbons, buttons, pressed flowers, cutters, reams of paper, strange devices for crimping, coloring pads, embossing guns, packing tags, cancelled postage stamps.

The middle of the room is filled with a table loaded with artist palettes, an Ott-Light for seeing close detail work, back issues of porcelain painting magazines, white china, and mismatched bottles—mineral oil, turpentine, alcohol. A trash can filled with old wrapping paper and discarded road maps tilts against the wall. A matted wool dog bed takes up the rest of the floor. The appliance surfaces are covered with cards in various stages of assembly. The washer lid is invisible. How did this happen? One conversation.

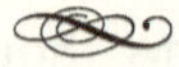

In math, a non-linear system is one where output is not directly proportional to input. Most physical systems are inherently non-linear in nature. Weather is one example. Simple changes in one part of a pattern produce complex effects over thousands of miles. The same holds true for human interactions. It's how my card making interest began in earnest.

In the crowded messy trailer that was the high school faculty room I dropped my satchel on my desk at the end of a long teaching day. One of my favorite colleagues was muttering about how much he disliked the commercialization of holidays and the expectation to send cards. It was May in the mid-1980s and Mother's Day was on his mind.

"Have you bought a card for your wife?" I asked. He launched into the reasons his answer was absolutely NOT. "It's all a Hallmark plot." Not wanting to argue, I changed the subject. But I didn't forget the conversation.

He did have a point about commercialization but Hallmark was not to blame. People have been marking special days, for mothers and others, since the Egyptians held festivals for the goddess Isis, the mother of the Pharaohs. I often told the story to my high school students of Julia Ward Howe's Mother's Day Proclamation in 1870. She was so distraught by the carnage of the Civil War she called for mothers to unite against such violence against everyone's sons. By 1914 Mother's Day was an official holiday. Since I always have felt parents in general are underappreciated it was a holiday I liked. But my friend was right about one thing. Cards were getting more expensive, as though price equated sentiment. I decided I could make Mother's Day cards for my mother and mother-in-law. They would be less professional looking, but more personal. How much time could it take to make two cards?

I finished the cards, sent them off, and realized how engaging the process had been. Making them gave me an extra few minutes to think about my mother and mother-in-law. I liked it—both the thinking and the doing. Maybe I could make more cards. There are lots and lots of holidays. *Chase's Calendar of Events*, the definitive book on the subject, lists more than 12,000. That was out of the question, but I figured if I left the supplies out, I could make cards whenever I had a few moments. As soon as we moved into a house with a big enough laundry, I was set. No one bothered my work. If there was one place in a house where my children and husband never went, it was the laundry room.

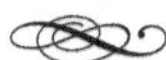

The popularity of handmade cards began with a Massachusetts woman, Esther Howland, who began selling handmade valentines in 1849. By the early 1900s they fell into decline, only to reemerge after World War I. By the 1980s, as I was getting interested, "alternative" cards, sent for no special reason, were beginning to appear. The timing was perfect—I didn't need a reason to send cards and now, making my own was appealing.

By the late 1990s card making, and its cousin, scrap booking, were enjoying a surge in popularity. I passed three shops selling supplies and offering classes on my daily commute. I began to sign up for evening workshops at a busy, cheerful store. Stamper's Warehouse, with its two classrooms always in use, aisles of supplies, and fleet of teachers, both local and traveling, was a mecca for women from all walks of life. At night I met nurses, lawyers, teachers, office managers, bank tellers, housewives, women caring for elderly parents during the daytime, wealthy matrons, grocery clerks, hairdressers. Some wanted to make cards to send to troops overseas. Others wanted to sell what they made. As different as they were, they loved the creative process. So did I.

Handling the paper, watching the instructors demonstrate composition techniques, and listening to my classmates at the long cluttered worktables sometimes was the most satisfying part of my day. It is very hard to tell if what we do as teachers or parents or even friends actually makes any difference. So much is elusive. Card making is a lot of things—not the least of which is—it's tangible.

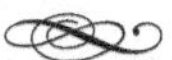

Richard Banks works for Microsoft Research in Cambridge, England. His title is "Interaction Designer" in the Computer Mediated Living Group. Most of his job is searching for ways to make digital things feel richer and more dynamic. His group is trying to create interfaces that fake gravity so we can turn them, flick them, and play with them as if they were real objects at the end of our fingertips.

In his book *The Future of Looking Back* he says, "The uniqueness of physical objects (as opposed to digital) makes them more fragile and, I admit, more meaningful." Banks begins by describing going through his deceased grandfather's battered suitcase with its collection of two hundred photographs and cards that were special to the ninety-four year old. Banks is forty-two. He figures at his current rate of taking about 5,000 photos a year, he will be leaving behind 200,000 images for his family…if they can find them.

Columnist George Will says cell phone cameras are so inexpensive and ubiquitous that photography has become a form of fidgeting. Facebook users upload 7.5 billion photos every month. The sheer volume reminds me of a poetry professor I once had who observed that if it took someone hundreds of pages to get their point across they didn't have one. I suspect Richard Banks knows that too.

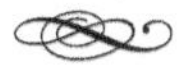

From the original two cards I've expanded to about 500 cards a year—a surprising non-linear outcome from one conversation. I give many as gift sets, and send the rest. The card-making supply stores are gone now, victims of a fickle economy and a world in which digital is the medium of communication and design.

I include with my gift boxes a note that says, in part:

I make my cards with many recycled items. My favorite embellishment is cancelled stamps with their special stories and mysterious travels. I like to think they are part of a long journey of connection weaving back and forth through time. W. H. Auden captured this movement in his 1941 poem "Night Mail":

This is the Night Mail crossing the Border
Bringing the check and the postal order.
Letters for the rich, letters for the poor,
The shop at the corner, the girl next door...
Letters of thanks, letters from banks,
Letters of joy from girl and boy,
Receipted bills and invitations
To inspect new stock or to visit relations,
And applications for situations,
And timid lovers' declarations,
And gossip, gossip, from all the nations.

I hope you enjoy sending these cards as much as I enjoyed making them for you.

Combining simple objects, connecting past to present, capturing cast-offs for new uses, leaving something for the future.
Border crossings.

A New Dance

A tarnished brass cup cowers behind other
forgotten relics in the dark cupboard.

The faded plaque whispers "American Legion Essay
contest—first place 1960—"Americanism today."

The girl who won is gone. She doesn't remember
what convinced the judges. What were we then?

She does remember the writing instructions.
How odd. Form, not substance.

"Breathe. Feet flat. Relax.
Keep tools close. Vary
Hand pressure. Find a rhythm.
Glide. Twirl. Spin. Move.
Chin up. Dance."

That was it! Form is part of meaning. How we do
what we do matters. It is part of us—but not all.

We were free. Independent. The woman wonders.
Is it still true?

The screen hums. Seductive. Insistent. The sound repeats.
Repeats. Repeats. Repeats.

Like a moth to light, she turns to answer. Her hand
clutches the mouse. Holds tight. Someone else is
leading this dance.

Are we still free?

Maybe.

Not.

Part Three

Eye Contact

"The common eye sees only the outside of things and judges by that, but the seeing eye pierces through and reads the heart and soul, finding there capacities which the outside didn't indicate or promise."
—Mark Twain

"The eye sees only what the mind is prepared to comprehend."
—Henri Bergson

FIRED EDGES

A surfing Madonna appeared just before Easter weekend 2011 in Encinitas, California. Artists disguised as construction workers affixed a striking mosaic of the Virgin of Guadalupe riding a wave to a wall under a train bridge. It technically was graffiti that should be removed under the law.

But the surfing Madonna's beauty drew a mass following. City officials spent thousands of dollars to hire an art conservation agency to find the best way to remove her without causing damage. Local opinion was split. Was it art or was it vandalism?

The answer is neither. It's the wrong question. Both art and graffiti are about communicating.

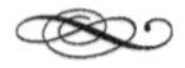

Jackson Pollock is an example. After repeated expulsions from Manual Arts High School in Los Angeles, he dropped out and moved to New York where he enrolled at the Art Students League. In 1945, in a rejection of what he called "the usual painter's tools," he began working on the floor. Dripping paint from a stick or stiff brush or pouring it right from the can, he began to work around the canvas, putting the full force of his body behind the flowing movements of his arm.

The result was a tangle that tracked the physical act of painting. He used unorthodox materials—industrial enamel, sand, gravel, and plumber's aluminum paint. As he worked, his cigarettes and the contents of his pockets spilled out and adhered to the tacky surface.

Although Pollock was initially misunderstood and rejected, eventually critic Clement Greenburg called him "the most powerful painter in contemporary America." In 2006 the highest price to date for a work of art, 140 million dollars, was paid for his 1948 "No. 5".

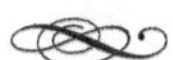

Human beings long for certainty and sharp distinctions. While crucial for air traffic controllers and surgeons, those distinctions are less useful in other undertakings, where nuance and subtlety matter more. Where multiple interpretations are valid. Art is one such messy place. Surprisingly, so is mathematics.

In 1931 German logician Kurt Gödel announced complete certainty was never to be encountered in mathematics by any route founded on traditional logic. The gist of his finding was that any standard of proof based on self-consistent principles of deductive reasoning is inadequate to establish the truth or falsity of every conceivable mathematical theorem. In short, there are always questions that cannot be settled.

His results stimulated the invention of non-Aristotelian logical systems. Aristotelian logic included, among other things, the law of contradiction (nothing can both be and not be) and the law of the excluded middle (something is either true or false; there is no third possibility).

The simplest of Gödel's frameworks is called a trivalent logical system, in which a statement can be true, false, or merely possible. His mathematical uncertainties are much as Karl Popper described science, as always having a tentative status subject to being revised, even drastically, by new discoveries. The same can be said of life itself.

Porcelain painters talk about edges. Hard edges mark boundaries. Soft edges are less visible, sometimes suggested with lacey or dotted lines. Good paintings include both. The best ones also incorporate lost edges where shadows match backgrounds and no visible line is apparent. Nature does this already. The rabbits in the field across from our house blend perfectly into the scrubby undergrowth. So do many other creatures. It is the human eye that fails to notice them.

Hard lines ruined many early porcelain projects. Over and over the teacher would exclaim, "Blend out the edges before you put your piece in the kiln. After it's fired we can't correct it." It took years before I got the message. In the same way, I am more convinced Socrates was right when he said, "The more I learn the more I learn how little I know." There needs to be room for wonder. Softer edges.

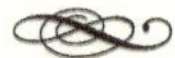

The Encinitas "surfing Madonna" will be taken down. It fills up public space. Never mind it honors the ocean the city celebrates as part of its identity. By most accounts the 10-by-10' foot rock and glass mosaic fills hearts as well. Inside a piercing blue wave she balances on a white surround, her vibrant green robe curling around her as she looks toward the sea. Down the mural's side are the words: "Save the Ocean." But according to city ordinances, it isn't art—it's unnecessary graffiti. Meanwhile, at the same time the Los Angeles Museum of Contemporary Art was unveiling a major show—"Art in the Streets"—the largest retrospective of graffiti in the United States. The irony is impossible to miss.

The line between yesterday and tomorrow doesn't divide life precisely in half. The past reaches forward. The future responds in ways we don't appreciate if we never look back. Fifty years ago Jackson Pollock took canvas off the easel and brushes off the canvas. In doing so he redefined the concept of painting. Graffiti artists are doing the same today.

In aesthetics there is one hard rule: No line should split a space in half. It is important in art. It is important in human relations too. It is a lesson I am still learning.

If the Encinitas bureaucrats are any indication, I am not the only one.

Off Kilter

Wandering through the stacks in the University of Oregon library during a break from tole painting in a study carrel I used once a week, thanks to my husband's faculty status, a book caught my eye: *The Mirror of True Womanhood: A Book of Instruction for Women in the World*. A new mother, I needed advice. The book, published in the late nineteenth century, didn't seem out of date when I considered many women I knew in our quiet Eugene neighborhood in 1972. Oregonians described themselves then with some pride as "at least ten years behind the rest of the country." Coming from Los Angeles, it seemed like more. Not that I didn't appreciate the skill and stamina homemaking required, but I felt unbalanced.

The book wasn't helpful. Neither were others stretched along the dusty shelf. It shared a call number at the Library of Congress with titles like: *Having It All: Strategy in the Sex Wars*, and *Help for the Hassled, Hurried, and Hustled*—which, in 1877, when it was published, was written by a man. The author, Reverend Bernard O'Reilly, was a New York priest who had been chaplain of the Irish Brigade of the Army of the Potomac during the Civil War. In twenty-two chapters with titles like "The True Woman's Kingdom: The Home" and "The

58

Wife's Crowning Duty: Fidelity," Father O'Reilly managed to stuff everything he thought a woman should know.

The bottom-line—"Women's entire existence, in order to be a source of happiness to others as well as to herself, must be one of self-sacrifice." If she failed she might end up like the selfish mother, en route to Europe, whose vessel was "wrecked amid the icebergs off the coast of Newfoundland," or the lazy housewife who suffered the even direr fate of having her disappointed husband "migrate to California."

When I think about it now I am reminded of writer Laurens van der Post, who wrote in his memoir of friendship with Carl Jung, "We live not only in our own lives but, whether we know it or not, also the life of our time." Father O'Reilly reflected his Victorian sensibilities, and perhaps nervousness as the world shifted beneath his feet. He ended his book by saying, "Men are born to be the providers in the home: they are formed by nature and still further fitted by education for every species of toil. The home with its quiet, its obscurity, is for woman: she is made to grow up in the shade."

As the woman's movement gained steam I was caught between the residue of nineteenth century expectations and the rising curtain of the looming twenty-first. I felt like someone trapped in the Star Wars IV garbage bay, where two sinister steel plates squeezed Luke and his friends closer to extinction minute by minute. The quick thinking of the little droid R2D2 saves the rebel heroes by disarming the power switch at the last moment. None of us had droids. We knew a way of life was vanishing, but we didn't know what would replace it. Many of my Oregon neighbors stayed put at home. I navigated into the working world, convinced that was the answer. For years I congratulated myself that I was balancing home and work so well.

Decades passed. I climbed the academic career ladder. Hunched at my desk late one gloomy afternoon at the high school where I was principal, I was trying to write my monthly newsletter column. I was exhausted. Out the window I watched a drug deal unfold across the street at a dilapidated motel, under a garish blue flickering sign. Not for the first time, I called the San Jose Police fast-response urban crime team. They were on speed dial.

"Okay," I thought to myself. "I'm on top of things. In charge. I've got the corner office, the secretary, the title, the position power, the salary, and the responsibility for the safety of hundreds of people." What I had lost was direct contact with students and any semblance of control over my life. Out of balance…again.

While much has been gained through the women's movement, much has been lost. Even Betty Freidan admitted things hadn't gone as she hoped. Marriages crashed, including her own. Children lost unstructured playtime—no one was home. Obesity skyrocketed as fast food replaced home cooking.

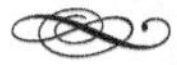

It is ironic that women characterize progress as moving into a male world; a world filled with as much stress and responsibility as exists at home. The grass isn't greener on the other side of the street. Every painter knows distance changes color. The backgrounds are muted, softer; the foregrounds sharper, easier to see.

Was it worth the sacrifices I made? I was never home and I missed it. Returning to my newsletter project I began reading a memo from the art teacher. At the top he had scrawled a quote from G.K. Chesterton—"If you look at a thing 999 times, you are perfectly safe; if you look at it for the 1000th time, you are in danger of 'seeing' it for the first time." The teacher was requesting field trip permission for a photography project. Chesterton wasn't talking about women and work, but I decided that afternoon it was time for a change.

I wrote my column that month on "Drawing Upside Down." It was a technique I learned in painting classes and used in writing classes. It dawned on me it would be useful for problem solving in general. We get caught up drawing 'generic' shapes, which are sometimes preconceived symbols instead of what is in front of us. Drawing and painting with the reference turned upside down forces us to see the shapes as they actually are.

The next month I announced I would be leaving at the end of the school year.

It was time to rebalance…again. Time to write a new chapter, colored less by social expectations and more by not just looking at my life, but seeing it.

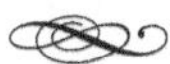

Pundits say "work/life balance" is possible with a little effort and planning. In my experience that is a denial of reality right out of "Titanic"—the scene where Leonardo DeCaprio's character is about to freeze to death in the North Atlantic, but first manages to mutter, "I don't know about you, but I intend on writing a strongly worded letter to the White Star Line about all this."

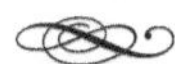

Turning away from what society acknowledged as "success" was harrowing, not impossible. It felt like waterskiing. To get out of the water you point the skis up, straighten your spine, bend your knees slightly for flexibility as you hit the rough spots, take a deep breath, fix your eyes on the horizon, and yell, "Hit it!" At the end of the run you let go of the towrope, spread your arms for balance, and skim along on your own toward shore. It's the best part of the ride.

I didn't have a droid to help me navigate my crisis of faith—in my career, my job choices, and my self image; but I did have a husband, who shouldered more so I could pursue goals for which the price was too high, the results too unsatisfying, the risks too great. Not risks to my marriage, but risks to me. A person who needed more space, more books, more time for projects, more time at home. It's the axiom

Joseph Conrad set down in *The Secret Sharer*: "We can never cease to be ourselves." I forgot.

In art, placement and balance work together to insure that no part of a painting pulls too much attention. Something else I had forgotten.

Bloomberg Businessweek reported in its January 9, 2012, issue that in 1970, 35 percent of women worked outside the home. Today it is 69 percent. Its cover was a large baby bottle with a man standing inside under the headline "The Perfect Husband." In the lower right it says, "He cooks, cleans—and lets his wife climb the corporate ladder."

Society has a new balance. History will decide if it was worth the price we paid.

Through a Paint Box Prism

I couldn't recognize the train wreck of my once-ordered life. Anxiety, a new unwelcome companion, destroyed my concentration. My mother's long hospice sojourn, together with disillusionment with a job that was supposed to be the pinnacle of my career, conspired to make me a case straight out of Mignon McLaughlin's *The Neurotic's Notebook*. In it he observed, "Love looks forward, hate looks back, anxiety has eyes all over its head." In 1999—me me me.

On impulse I decided to visit the local library. I hadn't stepped inside in a decade. Just another example of how distorted life had become, I thought. Disgusted with myself I paused by the statue near the front sliding doors. The bronze figure, a young girl, lies on her stomach, gazing into a book. The statue's title: "Forever Reading." Once that had been me. Focused. Engaged. Captivated by the artistry of storytellers.

The walkway was a crowded stream funneling young mothers clutching squirmy toddlers, jostling teenagers from the middle school across the street, senior citizens, city employees from the building next door. Everyone looking for something in one of the few places that has something for everyone. What was I looking for? I had no idea.

The lobby's left side was a wall of colorful Plexiglas sleeves like the grid from a giant board game. Pamphlets and flyers on the pulse of the city jockeyed with community college and adult education course offerings, tax forms, childcare agencies, tutoring programs for English learners, story time schedules, upcoming city council agendas, volunteer opportunities. There was nothing titled "for the disoriented and depressed."

Disappointed, I glanced at two large display cases stretching along the opposite side. Lined with black velvet drapes, they were filled with hand painted china: vases, plates, boxes, pitchers, portraits, serving bowls—arranged around a small sign:

> Student projects of porcelain instructor Ann Apperson. Beginning students need no previous experience. Learn the basics of design, mixing, and powder paints with an open medium. Kiln firing and registration available through the City of Pleasanton.

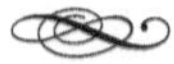

Painting was part of the landscape of my early married days. The concentration and focus it required had been almost as captivating as reading. I remembered those hours with my paints, stolen from the tyranny of daily demands, with a fondness burnished by the romance of distance. While I wasn't longing for the past, I was looking for something…something outside the mainstream, something absorbing. China painting seemed perfect…a glimmer of another time that somehow slipped through the cracks of yesterday, as out of place as unicorns and fairies. Which, I thought to myself, is one of the problems with the present. Excited, I left without a single book. I had an idea instead. I signed up for winter session.

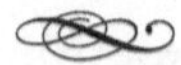

The first project was a peach study on a twelve-inch "chop plate."

The teacher talked about the botany of construction, made points about leaf size and growth patterns, and demonstrated on a Masonite plank. She explained paint mixing, wrote the colors on the white board behind her, then sat back to watch—like a harbormaster surveying boats approaching a dock. One by one we were called to her table where she asked questions and made corrections. Week after week I worked on the dusty red and yellow peaches, their deep green narrow leaves trailing haphazardly down the plate. Week after week she looked at my work, furrowed her brow, and sighed. "What is THIS?" she often snapped, pointing at some offending part of the design with the tip of her brush. Before I could answer she wiped off most of what I had concentrated on for the last hour in ten seconds flat. "Keep practicing."

Every week we sent our unfinished work home with the teacher, who fired the pieces in one of her four kilns. I always hoped something miraculous would happen in the firing, fixing my mistakes, but the pieces came back looking just as I sent them in. At the end of the term I showed my husband the peach plate that had occupied so many hours. Looking up from his desk he said, "Nice apples."

It was an inauspicious beginning. Or was it?

China painting and tole/oil painting are like badminton and tennis. Both sports use a racket and a net, but otherwise employ very different techniques. China painters move from light to dark; tole/oil painters do the reverse. China painters mix powdered paints; tole/oil painters use premixed tube colors. China painting has been in decline for two hundred years—fewer than 3000 painters are left worldwide; tole/oil painting remains popular with millions. Even the brushes are different—but there is one arresting similarity. They both require focus and concentration.

The term ended. I studied my project. It didn't look like any peaches I had ever seen, but I saw something else. I saw hours of dedicated work. Hours spent amid people creating something special from something ordinary—a common California fruit. Hours of having assumptions about what I thought I knew about painting challenged. Hours of learning. Hours of practice. Hours of...fun.

Vincent Van Gogh was a complicated man: a victim of epilepsy, an alcoholic, maybe made insane from the leaded paint he worked with. Fortunately for him, and us, Van Gogh was able to self-medicate. In the Philadelphia Museum of Art's "Van Gogh: Up Close," the introductory brochure says, "Focus on a small detail of nature allowed him to keep a calm frame of mind. Focus helped him put down the fires in his head."

He wrote about finding transcendence in a blade of grass. It's an image not unlike T.S. Eliot's writing in "Four Quartets": "We must be still and still moving/ Into another intensity/ For further union, a deeper communion."

Van Gogh's landscapes with their painstaking details of tree bark, groupings of irises, sunflowers, and vines brought him moments of peace. It is the peace most craftsmen and artists seek. Lucky ones find it. Maybe that is everyone's search. It has been mine.

Prisms disperse light into a spectrum or reflect light out. China painting became the prism through which I gathered the shards of broken dreams, and built a new shape. Twelve years have passed since that first winter class. My peaches look more like peaches now. There are bigger challenges—far beyond painting. Harder to solve, but easier to know where to begin. Start light, then adjust, then deepen. Don't overpaint. Works for most everything.

Through a paint box prism the world came back into focus.

TIME ARRESTED

FRAGILE. FLOWERS. I could read the bold words on the tall brown and green box leaning against the front door as I got out of the car.

Misty-eyed I maneuvered the long awkward shape to the kitchen. Behind the shipping label was a card—"To my daughter. Love, Old Dad." Inside were flowers—roses and lilies from my faraway 90-year-old father, sent for Valentine's Day. Among the many gifts he showered on the extended family, flowers were among his favorite. He sent them to all of us—for new babies, graduations, birthdays; for successes, for encouragement, for loss of beloved pets, for broken hearts.

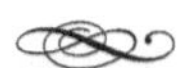

Dad had a standing order with a Virginia florist for deliveries to Mother's grave at Arlington National Cemetery for most holidays and her birthday. December was their anniversary month. Every year the florist sent pictures of beautiful red and green arrangements nestled against the white tombstone. A fifty-six year love story, still alive in flowers more than a decade after her passing.

Tucking the dozen multi-color blooms in the white ceramic vase included in the delivery, red hearts dancing around its base, I stepped back to admire my handiwork. The flowers brought both my parents into view as if they were in the kitchen with me. They were. They came in on the rose petals.

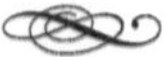

After my first china painting session ended I registered again. Soon I was signing up for the afternoon and night class. Wednesdays became synonymous with painting. I took a university academic appointment with the understanding that I wasn't available any Wednesdays. The routine was a metronome balancing two forces—a conventional activity people understood and a peculiar activity people overlooked. I didn't mind. In the first I was the teacher. In the second I was the learner. Learning made me a better teacher. It always does.

The painting instructor introduced new subjects every term. Landscapes, still lifes, birds and animals, vegetables, fruits and flowers of every variety—except one. Roses. No matter how often we asked she replied, "You're not ready." Eventually we chose our own compositions. Around the classroom people hunched over everything from enormous bowls to umbrella stands to lamp bases to small tables to dishware. Everyone had a favorite subject: holiday designs, portraits, horses, hummingbirds, exotic animals, water lilies, leaf studies—just no roses.

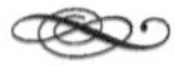

Six years passed. The teacher decided we had become "advanced beginners," capable at last of painting roses, the "queen flower" for porcelain artists. We tackled them first in a summer session at her home. Built in the 1920s, it was a *Wind in the Willows* sort of place with a steep roof and small diamond-shaped leaded glass windows. The narrow driveway—two parallel cement ribbons—led to the parking yard and weathered barn behind the cottage. Two blocks from Main Street, it had somehow escaped the present. It was a perfect setting for an old-fashioned art.

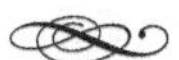

The four of us who gathered in the tiny "library" were eager to jump right in. But the first afternoon was devoted to sketching, listening, and simply looking at the beautiful roses that lined the narrow driveway beside the house. Scientists estimate roses have been blooming on earth for sixty million years, outlasting dinosaurs. Used for thousands of years for medicine, perfume, and cosmetics, Confucius wrote there were 600 books about roses in his Chinese emperor's library.

As I walked back and forth on the narrow drive, burying my nose in the parade of red, pink and yellow flowers bursting on bushes taller than me, I remembered the book of Isaiah promising in Chapter 35, "And the desert shall rejoice and blossom as the rose." My mind skipped on to Romeo's longing, "What's in a name? That which we call a rose/By any other name would smell as sweet." It was a speech I used to set up a debate on the power of words with my own students. In the summer sun the flowers needed no name. Their beauty spoke for itself.

We met every week that summer to paint roses—old ones, wild ones, dying ones, enormous open ones and tiny closed buds. Red for love, yellow for remembering, white for purity. The instructor showed us how, although rose varieties look different, they share a general shape in regard to outer petals. Some are more pointed, some are round, and some are very irregular. But if you look beyond the obvious, the shapes fit into three circles. Lightly sketching the perimeter, then painting the heart, turning it upside down to paint the shadow side first and then the light side, creates a foundation for the composition. It was roadmap for beginners. Taking something complicated and making it easier to understand was something I appreciated. It is something many teachers cannot do.

Once they master roses, some china painters never paint anything else. It is easy to see why. Their beauty, their fragile lives, their thorns… perhaps nothing else captures life so well. Taking time once a week to concentrate so completely on something so beautiful was just one gift of painting. Another was the link to what I saw as the longing of people to make their world more gracious, more beautiful, by growing a flower that speaks without words. The teacher planted her roses forty years before. The first one was a gift from her only child. The young boy who gave her the bush one Mother's Day was now almost fifty years old. But when she talked about her roses the affectionate son he had been was back.

France's greatest living poet, Yves Bonnefoy, wrote about Shakespeare, "I should say that, in his work, I see no opposition between the universal and the particular." In his own work he has devoted himself to what he calls the universal "here" and the eternal "now." Painters are devoted too—to using their tools and understanding of shapes and patterns to capture images too soon gone. They are images connected to their heart.

Bonnefoy wrote in *Passerby, These Are Words*:

And for you who now move on,
Pensively,
Here becomes there without ceasing to be.

From my father's house in San Diego to my doorstep in northern California or the quiet Virginia cemetery 3000 miles away, flowers bring the same message—across time and distance we are still together.

I paint rose compositions six or seven times a year. I give most of them away…my version of sending flowers. The projects are a way for me to be in the present and the past at the same time. I was wrong thinking my instructor's house was one time forgot. It wasn't forgotten—it was timeless. The greatest lesson that summer wasn't inside the house. I nearly walked right by it along the drive.

Knowing where to look. Harder than it seems. Always worth the effort.

GRAYSCALE NEGLECT

In 2012 the world (or parts of it anyway) was celebrating the 200th birthday of Charles Dickens. A wealthy woman who painted occasionally with us traveled to England to be part of festivities that included meeting the queen. An adventurous widow of extraordinary means, she had hosted the china painting class at her remarkable three-acre estate—filled with museum quality work on every wall and available surface. "I'm a collector," she said. Owner of several homes, by all accounts generous to her family, a patron of another painter I knew, trustee of a small college, I wondered if she understood the Dickens she was celebrating.

As most schoolchildren used to know, between the 1770s and the 1840s England was transformed from an essentially agricultural island into the most powerful industrial nation in the world. Machines appeared that revolutionized cotton manufacture—the steam engine, the water frame, the spinning jenny. Transportation networks—canals, roads, railroads—led to a migration from country to city overnight. What happened next—the rise of manufacturers and merchants to political and social power—resulted in the inevitable separation of "Heads of Industry" from "Hands that Produced." But human welfare didn't keep pace with material prosperity. No one wrote about it better than Charles Dickens.

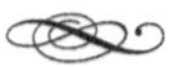

When he first saw grimy, dirty Manchester in 1838 he vowed to "strike the hardest blow in (his) power" for victims of exploitation in cotton mills. He did so over and over, never more than in *Hard Times*, the shortest of his books, but the most direct. In fictional Coketown, a wealthy retired merchant, Thomas Gradgrind, opens a school based on his Utilitarian worldview. A world obsessed with facts. A world where one character says, "I beg your pardon for interrupting you, sir…but I am sure you know the whole social system is a question of self-interest. What you must always appeal to, is a person's self-interest. It's your only hold."

In Simon Cullow's book *Charles Dickens and the Great Theater of the World,* Cullen writes, "He knew what poverty was. He knew what it was to be rejected, to be cast aside, to live in squalor." For Dickens the narrow focus on profit maximization and self-interest created an aesthetic blindness that squeezed all poetry and kindness from life. Beginning with *Oliver Twist* and its descriptions of the terrible plight of children, he became the most popular writer in England.

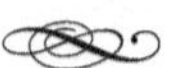

My graduate seminar "Social Foundations of Education" asked the question, "What do people value and want to see in their schools?" I began with Dickens' *Hard Times.* The novel, with its convoluted Victorian plot, ends with only one character achieving happiness—Sissy Jupe—the person least suited for a world where facts and figures held sway over the more humble ideas of faith and charity. The graduate students were troubled. They wanted to be part of a world with a broader agenda than economic, but they were being swept away on a tidal way of expectations and assessments that measured less and less with more and more accuracy.

Society told them what to measure, what to stress, what to value. It became all they saw. All they were allowed to see if they wanted to keep their jobs. They packed away their art supplies, music lessons, geography, history, philosophy, physical education, industrial arts. All we have left in public education is what society sees as the path to professional financial success.

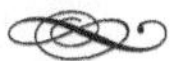

Painters talk about value too. It gives depth and dimension to compositions. Artists use it to describe the amount of light or dark in a color. The simplest way to determine a color's value is to imagine a color image run through a black and white copy machine. The result is a picture with all shades of gray from black to white. These are the values of the colors—the darker the color the lower the value. Color value is important because it helps create light/dark contrast. The darkest part of a painting helps bring the focal point to attention.

Understanding value was difficult. I couldn't understand why my colors were either too garish or too bland. Year after year, my projects seemed "off." I didn't know how to fix them.

One winter painting session the teacher chose pansies. With their two overlapping upper petals, two side petals, and a single wide bottom skirt with a beard coming from the center, they have a long popular history in art and with poets—who call them "love in idleness." After sketching the pansy around the inverted V that is the center, the flower is filled in with a middle-value color. Deep values are added behind the side petals. Wiping at the edges creates lighter values for ruffles. I couldn't do it. Eight frustrating weeks later, I joked to the teacher, "Looks like I failed pansies." She didn't disagree. For the next couple of years whenever anyone painted the colorful little flowers, I just groaned and looked away.

My "pansy failure" became a running joke. I relegated my unfortunate cracker tray, with its bright, sinister-looking pansy faces marching down the center, to the laundry room, where its offending design was hidden beneath a pile of card making tools.

Several years passed. One day the teacher said, "I have an idea. I think you need to focus on value. Let's use pen and ink to do a series of black and white projects. You'll get a better idea how 'value quality' helps."

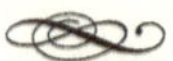

Using just black and white seemed odd when I had a paint box full of colors. The subjects seemed odder still. The teacher chose carnations, fuchsias, and birds for a set of small vases and trays. The pen was an unfamiliar tool, the projects complicated, the technique required attention to detail—something I had become less careful about.

Her plan worked. I began to see how high value contrasts controlled visibility, while lower value contrasts were calmer. I pulled out my college collection of tiny art books. I understood Rembrandt's light shapes on dark backgrounds and John Singer Sargent's middle-value contrasts in new ways. In a grayscale photo of a Claude Monet sunset it was hard to find the sun. Below it the writer noted, "This trick of value contrasts has been called the 'secret of the masters.'" The little books had been part of my library for many years, but I finally understood what I had been looking at all along.

On my own I returned to pansies. Not neglecting value made the difference. I seldom paint on china with gold edges, although most painters prefer it. I made an exception for a pansy study. I wanted the lesson to stand out. The flowers are soft, the design works. Along the left side I used the pen that helped me understand value to write, "There's pansies, that's for thoughts—'Ophelia in Hamlet.'"

When Facebook filed for its initial public offering, it revealed the combined pay of its top five executives—$83 million. It was the lead story in both web and print media. Two people will be billionaires. The same day a small article on page eleven reported new government figures—one in four children in America live below the poverty line. Forty-three percent of all children live in "economically unstable" homes. That news didn't cycle through the Internet at all.

Since his death in 1870 Charles Dickens' novels have never been out of print. In *Our Mutual Friend* he wrote:

> Mr. Podsnap settled that whatever he put behind him he put out of existence. Mr. Podsnap had even acquired a peculiar flourish of his right arm in often clearing the world of its most difficult problems, by sweeping them behind him.

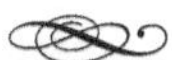

In painting I learned as long as I used only high-value contrasts, my work would be limited. Extremes created problems. Ignoring them didn't make them go away.

In *Hard Times* Mr. Gradgrind says over and over, "Facts alone are what is wanted in life." No deviation allowed.

Facts are important but they are not the only things. Dickens knew that. He wanted us to look into the gray. To see. To do something about the workhouse. The workhouse where, in another story, Bumble says, horrified, "Oliver Twist has asked for more!"

I often think about my former graduate education students when I paint—their dreams evaporating in a haze of regulations and constraints. I think about Oliver too. He is still asking for more. One hundred and seven y-four years have passed since his request.

I wonder how long he will have to wait.

Shape Shift

December clocks have a different rhythm. Instead of a measured analog "tick-tock-tick-tock," they move at the speed of my digital kitchen timer—numbers tumbling by in a blur. Every year Christmas comes sooner. I love Christmas. I love "keeping" Christmas. Why was it becoming more difficult? I pushed the nagging question aside until one recent year when the "invisible elephant" materialized on Christmas Eve—unexpected, unwelcome, and unavoidable—impossible to ignore any longer.

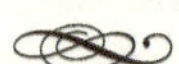

We celebrated Christmas at home, ever since navigating 600 miles between our two families became untenable with small children. Christmas Eve in northern California, Christmas Day driving to San Diego, Christmas lunch at the Bakersfield MacDonald's—not a good idea.

I invited everyone to our house. I made lists every November—bake, decorate, shop, wrap, entertain. My parents arrived the week before, my sister's family the day before. The days following we visited my husband's parents and family. Two weeks of cooking, conversation, catching up. The pattern repeated unchanged for decades. The pattern didn't change, but the family did. Parents died. My sister remarried, inheriting a whole new set of relatives. Children grew up, moved away, married. Some had children of their own. Gathering became more complicated. But we weren't the only ones changing. Society changed too. The old ways didn't fit. I pretended Christmas was exempt. It wasn't.

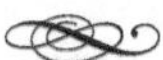

"Christmas" decorations began popping up before Halloween. Last year the box store in our neighborhood put up its first display Labor Day weekend. If a secular world didn't care much about the Christian part of Christmas, it did care about the sales possibilities. Several years ago the entire family was able to be in Pleasanton for the holiday after a four-year break I told myself was "temporary." I had been planning since August—just like the commercial world. In early December my neighbor confessed he had seen the "Rudolph the Red Nosed Reindeer" DVD with his children 103 times since October. Lowering his voice he said, "I'm starting to hate those reindeer." I sympathized but I had my own problems. Everything needed to be perfect. Christmas Eve arrived. So did the family. Many had come long distances. Most were stressed by their own issues, holiday and otherwise. All were exhausted.

Gathering for Christmas Eve grace, my husband struggled to say a prayer that included the divergent paths represented in the circle. Some Buddhist, some spiritual seekers, some Catholic, some hybrid Protestants, some too young to know. Looking at their faces—distracted, disinterested, defiant, devoted, none delighted—ages two to eighty-eight, I was discouraged. Jim was distraught.

He disappeared upstairs before the dishes were done, reappearing and disappearing the next day like the Cheshire cat. In the confusion no one seemed to notice. But I did. My "perfect" planning punctured—like Harry Potter's unpleasant Aunt Petunia after an unfortunate magic spell. We needed a different model. After Christmas I went grocery shopping at the box store. Not a single Santa, singing snowman, or ceramic Nativity remained. In their place loomed enormous red hearts and a sprinkling of pastel Easter bunnies. It was December 27. Time had lost its shape.

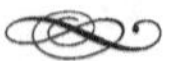

In painting the flow and line of the subject shape leads you through the piece. There are lots of rules about using an S curve or a C curve to design. They both give balance as well as make your eye follow a line through the subject rather than having a static non-flowing image. A single flower without stems or leaves in the middle of a plate would be lifeless—no movement. Your eye would lock in one place. Leaves, stems, and subordinate blooms along the curves create energy. Good designs lead your eye through the subject to the edge and back.

I began a January painting class while still packing Christmas away. The first session the teacher critiqued the complicated Dresden flower design I sketched. Her assessment: "No pathways. No connections to the center."

"That's it! That's what's wrong," I thought to myself. "Not wrong with the plate. Wrong with Christmas." Society lost the journey—the "before," the waiting, the anticipating, the centering—and zoomed in on the day itself. So had I.

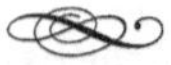

In the early 1890s, William Dean Howells published a little fable called "Christmas Every Day" in one of the most popular children's magazines of the time, *St. Nicholas*. Once upon a time, the narrator explains, "there was a little girl who liked Christmas so much that she wanted it to be Christmas every day in the year." She found a fairy to grant her wish, and she was delighted when Christmas came again on December 26, and December 27, and December 28:

After it had gone on about three or four months, the little girl, whenever she came into the room in the morning and saw those great ugly, lumpy stockings dangling at the fireplace, the disgusting presents around everywhere, used to sit down and burst out crying. In six months she was perfectly exhausted, she couldn't even cry anymore. [By October] people didn't carry presents around nicely anymore. They flung them over the fence or through the window, and instead of taking great pains to write 'To dear Papa' or 'Mama' or 'Brother' or 'Sister,' they used to write, 'Take it, you horrid old thing!' and then go and bang it against the front door.

These days, by the time Christmas rolls around, it feels as though this is very nearly what we've had: Christmas every day, or some faint version of it, since catalogs start arriving at the end of summer. Its shape is gone. Every secularized holiday loses the context it had in the liturgical year. Christmas has lost Advent. We have lost the time of genuine anticipation—the time before, the waiting, the Old Testament longing.

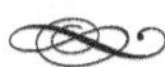

All that's left is more Christmas decorations. More lights. More food. More glitter. By the time Christmas arrives it feels like an afterthought, not a promise fulfilled.

Our adult children made the suggestion. Why not change the pattern? Why not look for chances to gather at other times? Summer? Thanksgiving? They were right. No one is the "keeper" of Christmas. It belongs to all of us. The next year we celebrated one of the best Thanksgivings in memory—together and focused back in the "picture"—not on the fiercer, wilder, frenzied burning of the long Yule season.

When painter Andrew Wyeth died in 2009 at ninety-one, his death provoked diverse reactions. Many in the art world praised him as one of the most significant American artists of the twentieth century. Plenty of others lumped him with Norman Rockwell as a mere illustrator, and dismissed his most famous painting, "Christina's World," as a "mandatory dorm room poster."

Rob Storr, dean of the Yale University School of Art, said:

> Wyeth was an anti-modern painter. He did paintings that never changed in a style that never changed. His image is one of stasis in a world that changed dramatically around him. It is in many ways a futile exercise, but he did it with great energy and conviction.

I like Wyeth. I like his patriotism, his sincerity, his New England roots. I also like his ability to have lived life out of contemporary time. He focused on what mattered to him, not what mattered to critics. As the painter Mark Rothko once put it, "Wyeth is about the pursuit of strangeness, but he is not whole, as Hopper is whole."

I doubt Wyeth thought his work incomplete. His paintings have the quiet movement good design creates—to the edges and back to the center of interest. The world has changed. The principle hasn't.

Christmas Eve is quieter now. My childhood memories are back. It is a time out of time. Last year the hours were unhurried, a gradual slow motion kind of day. Even the air felt different. I put the digital kitchen timer in the cupboard. My family was creating new traditions, new shapes, new memories, in new places—for an old story. A story of hope.

A story for the days after Christmas, not the days before.

I shall see him, but not now: I shall behold him, but not now.
—Numbers 24:17

Rebalance

Outside, drought weakened
the brittle trees, fading them
to sickly grayish-brown.

Inside, one lone faux fir—imperial,
emerald green, impassive—loomed.

It stood defiant, smug, pampered,
looking out the window at its
anemic cousins.

Stripping off its gaudy decorations,
I began tugging at its trunk.

It collapsed with a jerk like an
enormous umbrella.

The outside trees swayed in the wind,
nodding their approval.

Part Four

EDGING TOWARD UNDERSTANDING

"*There is an eternal landscape, a geography of the soul; we search for its outlines all our lives. Those who are lucky enough to find it ease like water over a stone, onto its fluid contours, and are home.*"
—Josephine Hart

"When I'm working on a problem I never think about beauty. I think only how to solve the problem. But when I have finished, if the solution is not beautiful, I know it is wrong."
—R. Buckminster Fuller

Good News Disguised

Sometimes we don't realize what we've learned until we've already known it for a very long time. Writer Ann Patchett says:

> Coming back to something can help you see how all the dots in your life are connected, how one decision leads you to another, how one twist of fate, good or bad, brings you to a door that later takes you to another door, which, aided by several detours—long hallways and unforeseen stairwells— eventually puts you in the place you are now."

For me one of those "somethings" was a tole project.

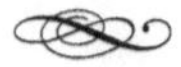

The most exhausting part of motherhood is the fact that for 99.9 percent of the various needs, you can't simply decide to "opt out," or even put them off until later; a child preparing to run into traffic takes precedence over anything else. It is the loss of the smallest measures of mental freedom and self-containment, the ability to pay attention to oneself when needed at that moment(!), that carries the most impact on our lives, energy, and sense of self.

84

At home I painted in the hours before dawn, before daytime demands. As I worked the room changed from black to gray as Oregon's oft-hidden sun announced a new day beginning. On Thursdays a widow neighbor watched the children. I took a paint filled tackle box to the University library. Using Jim's faculty status to reserve a small study room the size of a closet, I would set up my paints and lose myself in a landscape or still life. It was a routine very similar to my Whittier study carrel days. The difference was at Whittier I looked at the paintings tucked around me; in Oregon I painted them myself.

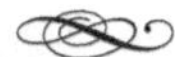

The National Society of Tole and Decorative Painters held an optional certification examination once a year. Submitted projects were evaluated on a long list of criteria, from brush control, to composition, to color choices, to wood preparation and finishing. I decided to apply. I spent months on my submission. The subject, chosen by the Association, was a formal still life. A copper cylindrical vase with daffodils, daisies, and poppies cascading out stands on a shadowy table. To the left grapes, strawberries, and a ripe peach surround a small oval decorated box. Muted yellows and reds filter through the background. I imagined it sat in a prosperous colonial dining room. It came to life in the bowels of the university library.

I wrapped the 11-by-17" piece as though it were glass instead of wood and sent it off to New York. Two hundred points was the qualifying score. I had been painting for some years and knew it was the best piece I had done. I was sure I would qualify. If there was anything I was good at, it was taking tests. When the critique arrived some weeks later I tore the envelope open. "We regret to inform you…" it began. As I scanned the evaluation grid phrases floated by, "needs more contrast…deepen shadows…doesn't shimmer." My score: 188. Close. Not close enough.

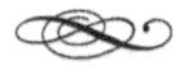

I jammed the project in the back of the winter coat closet—too discouraged to look at it for weeks. Never mind all I had learned in the process—the happy hours I spent in classes and in the library carrel, the people I met. It is disappointing even now to remember how disappointed I was then. I wasn't as resilient as life requires. Time taught other lessons that made this failure seem insignificant. But not then.

Dave Henderson was a Boston Red Sox back up player in 1986. He hit a home run that defeated the Angels in the seventh game and got the Sox to the World Series, where they lost to the New York Mets. Later Henderson said, "I actually won a World Series in 1989, but the one I think about most is '86. It hurts more to lose than it feels good to win." Yes, it does.

I continued painting and began teaching a beginning evening class at a large local craft supply store. Joyce Steece, the wife of another professor, was my first student. An English teacher, she was like me, not teaching in Oregon, looking for ways to keep learning. We talked about breaking painting into manageable parts and how similar that was to teaching someone to compose an essay. Before I completed a second submission, we left the Northwest. The Steeces returned to USC and Joyce to a long career, as did I. I often began my lessons on expository writing by painting a simple apple for class. It helped my students. I wonder if she did the same.

Today the colonial still life hangs on the wall. It looks the same as it did three decades ago—but the young woman who painted it is gone. I occasionally study it through the lens of the present. Three things stand out:

• Although I met the technical requirements, the painting looks stiff. Still lifes aren't still. My porcelain teacher says, "Make your work sing!" Though my project wasn't porcelain, it wasn't singing either. It was humming.

• The time I spent with other amateur painters was as important as the painting. After all, amateur descends from "amator," which is Latin for lover. Throughout much of its history it has also been used to refer to people who engage in an activity for love rather than money. Having enjoyed community concert bands and local theaters that dot the landscape, I know how useful a role the serious amateur of all kinds plays in community life.

• Most important, just because things hadn't gone the way I planned didn't mean they had gone all wrong. I became a better teacher and a better painter than I would have otherwise been. And because I was so unaccustomed to failure in competitive settings, it was a step toward becoming a better human being…or at least a more compassionate one.

Living has taught me, since those days, that there is a balance between getting what you want and being open to the things that actually come your way. There are many more important challenges than painting certifications—but in its time and place it was important to me. Today I think certification would have been terrible.

Life is not about getting certified. It is about remaining curious, staying open, trying not just one day…but every day. The real trick is to let life, with all its missteps and regrets, be always more alluring and mysterious than its end.

The twelve points I didn't earn gave me a chance to rethink something I thought I knew. The quiet cylindrical vase became a touchstone. When family issues loomed large, or teaching became overwhelming, I would sometimes stand in front of the wooden picture and think.

From a painting perspective my still life is quiet…barely "humming" in fact. From a life perspective, I hear it singing. It's a melody I recognize.

I wrote it myself.

THE COMPANY OF STRANGERS

Between the end of my discouraging high school principal-ship and before the Chapman University appointment the following spring, I decided I needed one thing—anonymity. Something meaningful I could do alone. Alone was key. No groups, no committees, no project teams, no political wrangling. An art class might be the answer. I was wrong. Not wrong about the class. Wrong about what I needed.

The china painting session began in January. Pulling into the crowded Community Center parking lot, I snagged the last slot, farthest from the building. The rain and angry gray slashing clouds turned noon into night. Soaking wet and grumpy, I ducked into the lobby. Opposite the glass entry doors the Center's fluorescent lights crisscrossed the art room ceiling like a giant tic-tac-toe game piercing the gloom. Dripping my way across the floor, I hesitated in the doorway. The smell of paints, alcohol, oils, and turpentine swirled out, taunting. Should I go in? Go home?

A break in the clouds sent shafts of light streaming through the skylight above onto tables below stacked with brushes, rags, design books, and blank china plates. A tiny Chinese lady looked up from her seat. "Come in," she said. "There's a place right here." Seven words. Simple. Short. Sincere. Stepping inside I thought to myself, "If this doesn't work out it's only eight weeks."

"I'm new. I'm not sure what to do."

"I'll help you," she said. "And the teacher will too. You'll see."

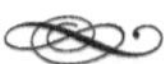

Her name was Mandy. Through that first winter and spring, she encouraged me, answered questions, loaned me supplies I didn't have. The mother of two young children, painting class was her 'time away.'

"Do you mind if we visit while we paint?" she asked. "I want to practice my English." Did I mind? What about my idea of being left alone?

I considered. What about the kindness she had shown me? After the lesson presentations, the dozen or so students worked independently as they waited for the teacher's help and critique. Most knew one another already, understood the basic techniques, and were involved with their own conversations. "No," I decided. "I don't mind."

It was the start of a trip with destinations beyond painting. I didn't expect to have much in common with a young Chinese mother thousands of miles from her home and culture. Something else I was wrong about.

Years later Jim and I attended a talk by the *Economist* writer Robert Guest. Held on the 47th floor of the massive San Francisco Bank of America building, the view of the city's famous lighted bridges was the perfect backdrop for the author's latest book, *Borderless Economics*. Some in the audience—consultants, business people, policy leaders—grappled with Guest's assertion, "We are all brothers under the skin." Not me. I wasn't thinking of trade implications or business prospects—I was thinking of Mandy and our long ago conversations about children, family, women's roles, loneliness in new places. I didn't have to read his book to know he was right.

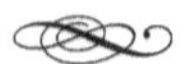

As the Wednesday painters spent hours together, laughing and struggling with projects, little pieces of our own stories began to trickle out.

Vera gave up an Ohio home she loved when her husband became ill. She moved "temporarily" into a room adjacent to his in a nursing home she hated. "Temporary" lasted seven years until his death. A cellist in the Cleveland Symphony, nursing home life sapped her creativity. The leave of absence she took for her husband morphed into her resignation when she moved almost immediately after his passing to Pleasanton. She began caring for her fifty-year-old dying son. Painting was respite time away from his bedside. She continued with it after his three-year struggle ended. The first eight-week session she returned she spread her paints out around her, and then sat motionless for the entire class. She didn't paint. None of us commented. The following term she brought a colorful blue and yellow paper napkin, pointed to it and said, "It's time to begin again. I'm going to paint these sunflowers. They remind me of home."

A coincidence?

Sunflowers were the emblems of the religious order that owned the school where I spent so many unhappy days as principal. In my office had been a large picture of them with a quote from the foundress, St. Julie Billiart, imposed over it. "Turn your face to the sun," it said. "God will always assist you." It was a coincidence I couldn't ignore. Vera's courage inspired me.

Three weeks before Vera died in her sleep at eighty, we visited a former classmate who had retired to nearby Manteca. Anita, a quiet Filipina neonatal intensive care nurse, worked the night shift in a San Jose hospital for years. On Wednesday afternoons she painted, on four hours sleep. I couldn't understand why she always looked so disheveled and tired. When she explained what her job was, I saw her in a different light. What looked like disorganization shifted to commitment.

Arriving back in Pleasanton Vera invited me in for a martini. "I still enjoy one every afternoon," she smiled. I'd never tasted a martini. It seemed impolite to decline. I offered a toast to her long life. "Thank you," she said. "I've been very lucky." Humbled, I knew "lucky" wasn't the word I would have chosen if Vera's story had been mine.

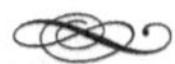

Gentle, white haired Bernadette raised five children, graduated from UCLA when Los Angeles was still a manageable town, and taught home economics. Slipping into Alzheimer's, she sat next to me for several years, entertaining us with stories of women's lives in the 1940s, until she disappeared into a world we could no longer visit and she couldn't escape.

Bernie was one of the few men who painted with us. Retired from Lawrence Livermore Labs, he was a taciturn engineer whose interest, besides oil and china painting, was a fierce dedication to restoring America's almost extinct chestnut trees. Bernie grew seedlings in his backyard, hundreds at a time. Every fall he would load his old Volvo, drive across country to meetings of the National Arbor Foundation, and deposit his treasured tiny trees.

Bobbie lived on an eighty-acre ranch, raising and training horses. Sometimes we painted at the ranch, surrounded by her memories of growing up at racetracks where her father had been a jockey.

Everyone had a story. They were unique, textured, funny, sad. The years unfolded. New painters joined the Wednesday group. Others moved on. We painted through the death of a spouse, divorces—their own and even their adult children's, job losses, problems with teen-agers, problems with elementary children, financial setbacks, new homes, health scares, family dramas. People would bring books they had read to share. Sometimes they brought food from their holiday celebrations…Eid, Chinese New Year, or Christmas baking. Often they remembered one another's birthdays.

On the surface we couldn't have been more different. The youngest of us was in her twenties, the oldest in her eighties. We had been or still were engineers, nurses, teachers, human resource and marketing managers, mortgage brokers. Some were wealthy; others struggled. Almost no one had been born in California. Some came from the Midwest or the East coast. I was born in Florida. Many were from much farther: Pakistan, India, the Philippines, China, Columbia. Some had children at home, some had no children, many had grown children. Some wore the traditional clothes of their homeland. Some wore pearls. In the evening class people came in their office clothes. Anita always looked suspiciously like she was in her pajamas.

The Best Canadian Film Award at the 1990 Vancouver Film Festival was a semi-documentary, "The Company of Strangers." The next year it was released in America as "Strangers in Good Company." It is the story of eight women on a bus, all but one elderly, who are stranded in a cottage when the bus breaks down. Strangers at the start, they tell stories from their own lives. In the process they realize they have more in common than they imagined. The variety and texture of their lives wasn't the same, but thrown together they found something they hadn't been looking for—the surprising unity their individual experiences created. It gave them the courage to persevere.

Seventeenth-century Flemish painter Peter Paul Rubens was a master who understood contrasting texture and used it in a storied career of religious murals, portraits, and hunting scenes. In his work texture created energy: soft long straight lines in clothes paired with more complicated curly beards or collars, smooth skin of voluptuous maidens against rough landscapes, austere cold marble draped with warm extravagant fabrics.

Texture is important for china painters too. Sometimes it is achieved by using raised paste to create actual dimension. More often it is done with brush techniques and tools: saran wrap, q-tips, mop brushes, erasers.

The teacher realized the differences in her students— their backgrounds, their painting skills, their interests. Most subjects she chose didn't appeal to everyone, but she chose them anyway. She wanted us to master texture—fur, feathers, water, rocks, clouds, grass. Rough and smooth. Opaque and clear. Someone was always grumbling. In the end, we became better painters for the effort it took to understand things we didn't think we needed to know. The bonus was spending time with people we wouldn't have encountered in any other circumstance. People who made the texture of our lives more interesting by sharing parts of their own. People who became friends.

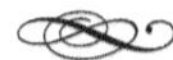

Fifty years ago John Glenn became the first American to orbit Earth in a five-hour mission that helped us feel better about the evil USSR's early lead in the space race. Glenn was a hero. The only rumblings were about the name of his Mercury capsule—"Friendship Seven." We didn't want to be friends with the Russians. Glenn is ninety now, still a hero. When asked about his ship's name in an anniversary interview, he said, "My children picked it. Turned out to be a good choice, didn't it?" It did. Children know many things grown-ups forget. I had forgotten friends come from all sorts of backgrounds, stations in life, ages. Or maybe it is something I hadn't known before my years in porcelain.

Whenever I see a hand painted piece, usually in a musty antique store, I wonder who painted it. I know they made their world more attractive. I like to think there were other benefits for them. I signed up for a painting class, but ended up with much more.

I hope they did too.

*"The sky was as Prussian blue as Potsdam could require, but it was
yet more like that lavish and glowing use of the color which a child
extracts from a shilling paint box."*
—G.K.Chesterton

LIVING COLOR

It was a destination birthday party—an important birthday—a 50th birthday. Winding along the rural roads of Sonoma County on a sunny afternoon, we saw countryside dotted with shabby cottages, mom and pop businesses, roadside vegetable stands. Wide swaths of vineyards crisscrossed the landscape like giant checkerboard lines.

Down a bumpy dusty narrow lane a house emerged out of the hillside. A beautiful, elegant Craftsman, it should have been out of place amid its more modest neighbors, but it wasn't. The wraparound deck, filled with revelers, looked across the valley to distant hills wearing rows of grape vines like exotic jewelry. Other guests wandered the grounds. This must be how Gatsby felt when he looked across the water, I thought. "The largest of the banners and the largest of the lawns belonged to Daisy Fay's house." Fitzgerald's world had its own surprises—so did the house before me.

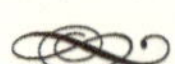

The host, the husband of the man whose birthday we were celebrating, took us on a tour. The colors were warm, subtle, muted. Both men had demanding jobs. I knew enough about color to know

94

these had been chosen to create the restful, quieting influence browns and greens elicit. The sightlines and room dimensions were precise. Turning a corner, I found a spectacular large, exuberant many-colored canvas. Against the measured subdued backdrop it was even more captivating. An attractive woman, wearing the turban that said she was fighting cancer, stood nearby. "Do you like it?" she asked.

"It's staggering. It looks alive." I said.

"It is alive," she smiled. "I should know. I painted it."

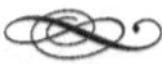

Tole painters select a color scheme as one of their first determinations in developing a design. China painters reverse the process. They focus first on the design—using color to reinforce it. Either way requires a knowledge of color theory—something I knew nothing about early on—a fact not obvious in my finished work because I pestered teachers to tell me what colors to use. It was a handicap beyond painting.

Decorating from scratch is like facing blank canvas. Color schemes came and went, in ways I never understood. In the 1970s everything was "harvest gold" and "avocado green." I dutifully set about staining unfinished wood in colors I saw in magazines and department stores, scouring yard sales, replacing carpet. As I was priming the rural mailbox I intended to paint green—not for mail, for storing bread on the kitchen counter—a senior professor's stylish wife paid her first visit.

"I see you like green and gold," she said. Actually, I didn't; but magazines said I should. "Too bad," she continued. "The new colors are colonial blue and burgundy." University communities can be small worlds. I didn't want to be out of sync. Bad form. Discouraged, I called a department store that offered "complimentary interior decorating evaluations."

I cleaned and polished every green and harvest gold surface, wondering why it was called harvest gold when it looked like hotdog mustard yellow. "Out of style. We'll see about that," I thought. The woman arrived, clipboard in hand. Colonial blue dress. Burgundy shoes. She strode from room to room like a general inspecting troops. Forehead wrinkled, lips pursed, she made small huffing sounds as she wrote. Finished, she cleared her throat. "One word comes to mind seeing your home." She paused for effect. "Insipid."

"Call me when you are ready to redo…everything."

Insipid? I wasn't sure what the word meant but I knew it wasn't a compliment. I checked the dictionary. It said, "Without distinctive, interesting, or stimulating qualities. Vapid. Dull. Uninteresting." I had to admit it was a good choice for avocado green. I knew what I didn't like: avocado and harvest gold, always feeling out of step, chasing fashion trends someone else decreed. I was less sure what I did like.

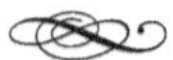

I began studying. No two people see color the same way. It is a visual sensation. Even your left eye sees different from your right. I enrolled in a color theory course based on the work of a decorative arts master painter, Ann Kingslan. For months we focused on color schemes—monochromatic, analogous, complementary, split complementary, double split, triadic. We applied the concepts in a polychromatic painting using all the colors called "The Vegetable Cupboard." Squash, peas, carrots, parsley, beets, peppers, eggplant, mushrooms, radishes.

The light we perceive as originating from the sun contains all the colors and is actually white. We created our own color wheels. We learned about color "families." I began to appreciate what happens when opposite colors on the wheel are mixed—you get gray. I began to understand the psychology of color, the seasons of color, the religious symbolism of Pennsylvania Folk Art—red for charity, blue for truthfulness, purple for sorrow. More important, I began to develop my own sense of how I wanted to use color in painting and at home.

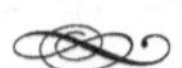

A chance visit to the Art Institute of Chicago several years later brought me face to face with Georges Seurat's "Sunday Afternoon on the Island of La Grande Jatte." I was mesmerized. Every color in the rainbow danced across the large canvas. Ladies with parasols strolled in the sun, children and puppies played on the grass, sailboats moved along, men lounged in the shadows. Seurat, a student of color theory, decided if he used miniature dots instead of brush strokes an optical illusion would merge them into single, more vivid images.

He worked on the canvas for two years. In the process he became the father of pointillism. The color and vitality captured what I was looking for—a celebration of life in many colors, not just passing fads. Today a 4-by-4' print of the painting is the focal point in our dining room. The room is the setting for many gatherings, the picture an invitation—"Come in. Your color adds to our story. Welcome."

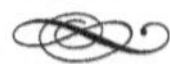

The Pantone Color Institute is considered the global authority on color. They establish the standards for its use in manufacturing and printing. Their Color Matching System means a shade of blue used in fabric in Brazil and wall paint in the United States will match exactly. Their job is to figure out the collective color mood of the world. When they do, it is announced in the form of Pantone's Color of the Year. In 2012 Tangerine Tango danced into the spotlight. That means people will see it in everything from accent walls to furniture to clothing.

Leatrice Eiseman, Pantone's spokeswoman and instrumental person in the selection process, studied psychology before coming to work at the Institute. About tangerine she says, "The color is more complex than red—with a 'come-hither' attitude." Magazines are showing tangerine knobs and pulls, bathtubs, kitchen counters.

I have studied color psychology too. Orange also produces hyperactivity. Do people really want hyperactive kitchen counters? I suspect the long-ago decorator I called is pushing orange disguised as tangerine this year. Someday Pantone will get back to avocado. And everyone will follow. After all, in 2009 they chose Mimosa, which looked like yellow and arrived on the heels of Michelle Obama's citrus inauguration suit. A symbol of optimism, it washed over the country. By 2010 it was out of fashion.

G.K. Chesterton is the creator of what is regarded as the second most successful detective creation in English literature after Sherlock Holmes—Father Brown. The fifty-three stories featuring the peculiar cleric are famous for many reasons: not only for the character he created, but his use of color in creating word pictures. Opening any story the reader finds poetic writing: "The evening daylight in the streets was large and luminous" ("The Man in the Passage"); "He was called by his intimates Mulberry in apt allusion to something rich and fruity about his dark rotundity and rather empurpled visage" ("The Vampire of the Village"). The brilliant description is not surprising. Chesterton was a talented artist trained at the Slade School of Art, one of the most important schools in the world in the late nineteenth and early twentieth centuries.

He was also a student of human nature. In "The Queer Feet" he says, " In the heart of a plutocracy tradesmen become cunning enough to be more fastidious than their customers. They positively create difficulties so that their wealthy and weary clients may spend money and diplomacy in overcoming them." He wrote that in 1911. Many things have changed the last hundred years. That has not. Sadly.

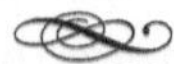

The 50th birthday party celebration continued into evening. I sought out the painter to learn more about her and her color choices. Her name was Terri Hill. "I was a graphic designer for three decades," she said.

"I began painting fulltime on New Year's Day, 2009, after my cancer diagnosis. Painting helps me appreciate every minute. I like unusual vantage points and rich, saturated colors. Red and green are complementary in the picture you like. Red is exciting, healthy, warm. It's a symbol of resilience. Green is hopeful."

Terri Hill chooses colors based on her knowledge of art, design, and emotion. So did Georges Seurat. So did F. Scott Fitzgerald.

Gatsby believed in the green light, the orgastic future that year by year recedes before us. It eluded us then, but that's no matter—tomorrow we will run faster, stretch out our arms farther…And one fine morning—

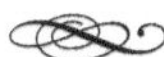

In Pennsylvania Dutch folk-art green is the color of eternal life, the color of renewal. Fitzgerald ends *The Great Gatsby*, "We beat on, boats against the current, borne back ceaselessly into the past." But there is a way forward. It's Gatsby's green light. Spring comes. With it the colors of the rainbow burst out.

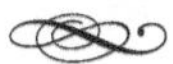

We live in a community with many Hindis. They celebrate Holi, the throwing off of winter gloom. Neighbors rejoice in the liveliness of a new season on the day of a March full moon. It is a festival of fun and merrymaking. People decorate each other's faces and clothes with colored chalk—every color on everyone. For one day there are no castes, no barriers between people.

Many Christians dye Easter eggs. We do. Celebrants wear white robes on Easter Sunday—the color that contains all in one. No barriers.

Georges Seurat, G.K. Chesterton, Terri Hill—different mediums, different generations, different styles. All with the same love for color and its power. Power to soothe and shape. Power to catapult, console, connect the human experience.

I don't need a decorator these days. Ours is a house of many colors. Many more are in my paint box. There are thirty-one variations of green—even avocado.

Celebrating life. In every shade.

October Coloratura

The damp snapping wind ices the bones
through to marrow.

Puddles from silver rain earlier in the week
create a chain of lakes
along the moss-edged cement sidewalk—
a mottled white ribbon
stained with silhouettes of
dying leaves like dusty chalk outlines
at a murder scene.

Soon their shadows disappear as more
and more descend, burying the decayed
charcoal shapes beneath soggy piles,
as though remembering summer's splendid
verdant canopy is too painful to recall.

The stern old trees rise from the
blotchy grass, shaking their black
limbs like fists against the cold
bitter blue sky.

Canadian geese peck at fallen brown
apples near the sleek granite building.

Winter is stalking the campus.

Autumn begins with the same three
colors: green landscape, yellow
leaves falling through a
gray afternoon.

—Notes from Ann Arbor, 2009

EARTHSHINE

"There is nothing like looking, if you want to find something. You certainly usually find something, if you look, but it is not always the something you were after."
—J.R.R. Tolkien

"Lost, yesterday, somewhere between sunrise and sunset, two golden hours each set with sixty diamond minutes. No reward is offered, for they are gone forever."
—Horace Mann, 1796-1859

Time and Materials

The door to the cramped office was locked. The appointment card read 3 p.m. The wall clock in the waiting area said 3:10. We knocked. With a jerk, it flew open. A man stepped out. Dressed in a black suit, white shirt, pale tie, he looked out of place amid the careless exuberance of a college campus.

"Come in," he said with a reassuring, jovial smile. "Sorry about the locked door. Human resources rules, you know. Let's start. You have an hour. Don't want time to get away."

He slid his business card across the table: "Retirement Planning."

The computer behind him ticked off the minutes like a basketball scoreboard clock. He had questions. "What do you need?" "What is essential?" "How much time remains?" The first two were easy. The last unanswerable.

Sixty minutes later we made our way across campus in the gathering gloom to the car. Where had the time gone? Not the hour, the decades. I found myself thinking about Mrs. Merrifield's lamp.

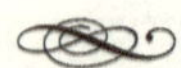

I was twenty-two. It was our first apartment. The previous tenant, a gentle white-haired woman, was moving to a retirement home.

She left behind one table lamp in the center of the living room floor. Attached was a note in a spidery hand. "Consider this a gift."

The lamp was like Mrs. Merrifield herself—the green and gold base worn and faded, the shade not quite level. But it worked. It was the first household item we owned. Years passed. More lamps appeared. Mrs. Merrifield's gift, outclassed and obsolete, ended up in the trash.

According to the black suit, the things we accumulated might be difficult. A minefield to manage. To maintain. I didn't think so. Material things aren't the problem. Knowing when to let go is the problem. I learned that from painting. Time was another story.

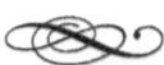

I acquired a large collection of books and magazines on arts and crafts over the years. The china ones often begin with lists— "Materials Used for Painting on Porcelain." What follows are forty or so items before they get to kiln requirements. Catalogues offer as many as sixty different brushes. Hundreds of colors. Thousands of blank objects to paint.

China shows and exhibitions feature earnest sellers offering a dizzy array of items "painters can't do without." I ended up with potions, bottles, boxes, tools I couldn't identify, much less use. Vendors extolled the virtues of one color "house" over another.

I bought vials from many. Soon I had fourteen rose shades, twenty reds, nineteen browns, even six grays. I couldn't keep track. Lugging my supplies to class took several trips.

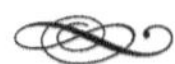

After painting for some years I stumbled on an instructional video on the Internet by Barbara Duncan. Duncan, a world-famous oil as well as china painter, was demonstrating "peace roses." What surprised me was her palette. Nine colors. She mixed everything from them. She used three brushes—a squirrel shader with a flat square top, a long thin scroller, and a small berry brush. "Of course, these take practice," she said. "Don't be discouraged. Keep on." She was talking about roses. I was thinking about tools.

I reduced my painting supplies by half. It was easier to carry, to choose, to create, to clean up. I experimented. I improvised. I deviated from suggested design palettes.

Theodore Geisel, aka Dr. Seuss, wrote his famous *Cat in the Hat* with 236 words after reading a 1954 article in *Life Magazine* asking why children's stories were so complicated. Afterwards, his publisher, Bennett Cerf, bet him fifty dollars he couldn't write a story with fifty words. Cerf lost. Geisel wrote *Green Eggs and Ham*. It remains one of the four best selling children's books in the world. Less became more.

Michael Masterson and Malcolm Gladwell are contemporary writers about achievement. Masterson says it takes at least 1000 hours of practice to get past incompetence in anything. At 5000 hours one becomes competent. He agrees with Gladwell's assertion in *The Outliers*—mastery comes after 10,000 hours.

2010 marked ten years of china painting. Ten years: to borrow from Pascal, nearly nothing in relation to infinity, nearly everything in relation to nothing. By Masterson and Gladwell's reckoning I am a little more than halfway to competence as a china painter.

How much time do we have left? The man in the black suit, surrounded by actuarial tables and charts, couldn't be sure. Nor could his locked door keep time from slipping away like pale winter sun on a cloudy afternoon.

Sort. Simplify. Substitute. Good advice for painting. For writing. For the material world. Time is different. There will never be enough.

Artists and writers don't stop time. They do make it easier to see it. With fewer tools I concentrate on what I am painting, not what

I am painting with. I waste less time rummaging for lost items. I've gained more—time to revisit favorite subjects. Reread favorite books. My paint box is lighter. My house is cleaner.

A man in black asked questions. A painter had some answers. Reduce. Restrict. Refine.

A poet had the rest:

> The painter Harlan Hubbard said
> that he was painting Heaven when
> the places he painted merely were
> the Campbell or the Trimble County
> banks of the Ohio, or farms
> and hills where he had worked or roamed:
> a house's gable or roofline
> rising from a fold in the hills
> trees bearing snow, two shanty boats
> at dawn, immortal light upon
> the flowing river in its bends.
> And these were Heavenly because
> he never saw them clear enough
> to satisfy his love, his need
> to see them all again, again.

—Wendell Berry
Sabbath XV, 2005

RISK AND REWARD

No silence is as uncomfortable for a teacher as the space between question and answer. We imagine our discussion starters will lead to waving hands as students jump in, eager and prepared. When that doesn't happen, most of us answer our own questions. Research says we wait less than a second when we'd get better answers if we waited between three and seven. Seven seconds? I wasn't willing to risk it. Seven seconds in a high school classroom is an invitation to chaos. I asked and answered so many of my own questions I felt like an actor playing twins… first one personality, then another. Lindsey Lohan reprising the Hayley Mills role in "The Parent Trap" had nothing on me. The routine left me exhausted, students bored observers.

I had two problems. First was the idea that an easy question with quick answers was learning. It's not. It's recall—something useful but different. The second was my aversion to empty space. After too many years of lessons that looked like game show preparation, through trial and error my questions improved. I stopped asking for short, recall responses in favor of those that required actual thinking.

A math teacher helped me with the space problem.

I began teaching in a school that used teacher peer review. A math instructor asked me to observe him. He chose "the difference between nothingness and nothing" for his algebra class. I listened to his lesson.

He began by holding his hand straight out in front of him, fingers spread apart like a determined school crossing guard. "What do you see?" he asked. Students smirked.

"Your hand."

"What else?"

"Your fingers," they said.

"What else?"

The class grew uneasy. "What about the space between my fingers?" he prodded.

"There's nothing there," someone called.

Beaming the teacher said, "Correct. And that's today's topic. Nothing"

The students were intrigued. So was I. It gave me an idea. Not about his teaching. About my own. Maybe space and silence weren't a problem. Maybe they were an asset.

At least fifteen hundred years ago nothingness found its place in arithmetic as the number zero. Trivial as it seems, it enabled us to express numbers more clearly and easily than ever before. A thousand years later nothing made its appearance in arithmetic, and it was not anything like nothingness. Nothing was named the null set. It represents in arithmetic what a virgin canvas and blank sheet of paper represent in painting and writing: latent being. With the null set, mathematicians have been able to show how every number known in arithmetic can be created out of nothing.

I began to think of the lag time between questions and answers as a null set. The gap became an asset. When they had time to think, to create, to test their ideas in their heads first, student answers extended discussions. They owned them. They defended their ideas.

I began insisting on space. I was no longer the single actor playing multiple roles in a slow movie. We might be uncomfortable, but no one was bored.

In painting I faced a similar problem. I didn't appreciate empty space. Every china blank made me long to fill it up. Classes focused on "subjects"—not on emptiness. Every project became a playground for not only what I was painting, but for techniques I learned. The more techniques I encountered, the more cluttered the paintings became.

After five years painting porcelain, I signed up for a one-week seminar with a traveling teacher. Her topic was morning glories. We painted eight hours a day. The blue and maroon flowers exploded across a 16-by-16" serving tile. Larger than most things I painted, I was intimidated by the space. I added border scrolls, lattice designs, dots, and dashes. They looked like garden pests chasing the flowers. I told myself they were whimsical. I filled up every empty inch.

The instructor raised one careful eyebrow. "Your subject shape is good. But you've forgotten the shadow shapes and negative space where there is nothing. Without them your work suffers. Stop concentrating on the subject. Look beyond it."

The next day she brought three separate flamingo pictures: a flock, two facing birds, and four birds looking left with different neck poses. She also brought a poster on which she had written:

EXCLUDE THE UNNECESSARY—"Be ruthless in eliminating any color, texture, line, value, shape, size, or direction that does not express the subject."—Edward Whitney.

We debated the bird pictures. Using Whitney's criteria the four birds was the powerful image. Beautiful negative shapes appeared around them. Whitney, an American watercolorist who died in

1987, was famous for explaining how to put any design, any subject, any style, on any surface and create a unified image. After his death one student wrote about a workshop she took with him, "I started to paint instead of just applying paint to paper." The morning glory workshop was that turning point for me.

Every day began with a photo analysis. One day the opener was two pictures titled "Pink Flowers." The first was a green lawn with an azalea border. The second was a close-up of several blossoms against a muted background. We got better and better at recognizing the power of selection, the power of space. "Including everything you see is easy," the teacher said. "The lawn and flower picture should be called 'Garden.' The flowers are secondary. Decide what the focus is, then make it happen. Don't weaken or distract."

I started a new morning glory tray—no scrolls, no borders, no clever dots and dashes. Added shadows. Used negative space. My flowers were no longer being harassed. Neither was the viewer.

It was a risk. Risking something I was comfortable with for the reward of doing something different. Something better. Something with more room—to breathe, to grow, to flourish with fewer obstacles blocking the way.

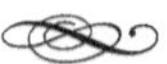

Nothing has become increasingly important for me. It is the space where ideas pop up, problems find solutions, worry recedes. Creative energy, like nothing, isn't anything if it isn't potential. It is one of the best parts of being alive. In this sense the human mind is the real null set; the mathematical version is a subordinate entity created after the mind's self-image.

Most of us value "busy" above all else. Busy equals productive. Busy equals important. There is another way to think about it. Busy can disguise, deflect, distract, delay. When people call me they often ask, "What are you doing?" If I say "Nothing," they plunge ahead. But nothing IS something. Without it math doesn't work. Paintings suffer. So do people.

John Updike said, "What art offers is space—a certain breathing room for the spirit."

Morning glories remind me.

Too Soon Gone

Jill Kinmont Boothe was a U.S. champion skier when she graced the cover of *Sports Illustrated* in 1955. The issue was still on the newsstands when she crashed during a race. A broken neck paralyzed her. She died February 9, 2012, at 75. Her life became a role model for the tenacious pursuit of altered dreams.

She learned to use her neck and shoulder muscles to write and paint, studied German and English at UCLA, and was a teacher for three decades. In 1975 she was the subject of a film, *The Other Side of the Mountain*. Everyone confronts obstacles, though most not as daunting as Boothe's. Some, like her, overcome them. Many more do not. Those that do are a privilege to know. A crew of painters, house painters, showed me.

Courage. Not on the ski slopes. At home.

Home ownership is trench warfare against decay. The house always wins. After sixteen years of benign neglect, ours was looking shabby. The "to-do" list grew longer…torn screens, cracked cement, broken appliances. Peeling gutters were the last straw. It was time to paint, patch, punch up the place.

Our experience with contractors ran the gamut from talented to terrifying. On one end were the unemployed History graduates who parlayed building skills learned from their fathers into an unexpected career. At the other end was the Samoan who tore up our yard in a landscaping project and then disappeared. The place looked like an enormous burial ground for voracious mutant rodents for months. We figured our batting average was a little under 50 percent for good work, on time, and within budget.

The peeling gutters evolved into an expansive project…outside, inside, doors, trim…everything nailed down got painted. A rotating three-man-sometimes-four-man crew was on site for a month. Their English language skills ranged from little to none. The company, Final Coat Painting, advertised "professional application and finishes." The owner spent several hours studying the house. "We'll spend the first week getting ready," he said. "Washing, sanding, filling cracks, masking." I interviewed four companies. He was the only one who talked as much about preparation as painting. I had learned through many failed projects and mediocre school lessons preparation makes the difference—in art, in teaching, in everything. They got the job.

Dressed in white, the men arrived on time, worked hard, treated their tools with respect, tidied up every night. They cleaned their brushes as carefully as I cleaned mine. Rooms were dismantled. Reassembled. Plastic covered everything. The place looked like a rock concert aftermath. Light fixtures drooped, furniture huddled together, windows disguised. I was fascinated.

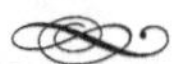

Rick, the English-speaking foreman, was in his mid-twenties. He was a good manager and a talented painter. Every morning he huddled with the crew like a basketball coach before a game—giving directions, solving problems, answering questions. "I didn't really like school," he said. "I like painting. Painting cars, actually. But houses are interesting too." I knew public school let Rick down. He succeeded in spite of it. No excuses. Determined. Focused. He didn't fit the "delayed adulthood" phenomenon sociologists write about. I admired him.

I sometimes ate lunch with the crew. Sitting on tall paint cans in the garage, we looked like diners in search of a table. They were people for whom daily life was an obstacle course. Loneliness. Discrimination. Language. Loss. They came from Mexico City, Guadalajara, El Salvador. Different places. Different cultures. In many ways strangers to one another.

The "fourth man," Luis, was different. He didn't always come, creating chaos as the others scrambled to do his work and their own. He complained…about the wife he married when she was fifteen, his four kids, his landlord, his welfare checks. He bragged about his flat screen TV, his pool table, his painting skill, his truck. I discovered he couldn't read. Worse, he didn't want to learn. His breaks were longer. His work was slower. The crew chose different music every day. He didn't like any of it. Soon after the project ended, he was fired.

The painters sometimes paused to watch me work at my paint table. I watched them too. They were artists on a big canvas. Up and down. Back and forth. Large sweeping strokes. Small delicate ones. We encouraged each other. I asked their advice about colors. For the house. For the china projects. At the edge of poverty, they refused to give up. Despite the long hours and backbreaking work, they were cheerful—kidding each other about food, soccer, weekend plans.

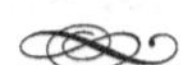

On the Friday before Mother's Day the crew was teasing Sal, a serious bespeckled father of two who concentrated on detail work—inside window frames, corners, hard-to-reach places. He didn't have a gift for his wife. The others either weren't married or had shopped. Sal admired the painted china. He studied the plates in the wooden hutch as he gently took apart the dining room. In the middle of the long table was a three-tiered porcelain serving tray. Painted red geraniums and fan shaped ruffled leaves wound around a gold center pole.

I paint geraniums because they remind me of Mother, who had a bank of them at the back of their Chula Vista property. She liked to sit on the patio and admire the cheerful colors in the warm southern California sun. "What a perfect gift for Sal," I thought. Something for his wife on Mother's Day—in memory of my own.

"Do you think your wife would like the centerpiece?" I gestured.

Eyes twinkling behind his glasses, a smile lit his face.

"Then it's yours," I said.

It was the crew's final day. We didn't speak the same language in words. We understood each other in paint. The trucks pulled away, hands waving out the windows like a parade passing. The transformed house the only clue they had been there.

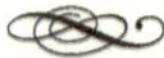

The International Porcelain Artists and Teachers publish a magazine six times a year. Evaluating the composition of a series of projects last spring they concluded, "Conflict adds interest. Too much conflict causes chaos."

That is as true for living as it is for painting. The conflicts that dogged the house painters' lives could have created sullen, unproductive, despondent people. It didn't. All but one adapted, adjusted, accepted the challenge of beginning anew.

Kinmont Boothe said in a 1967 interview, "To get mad doesn't get you anywhere. You sort of look for what's good that's left." The house painters voiced the same sentiments, in a combination of languages, gestures, and smiles.

The men are gone now. Time stole them away. Every day I see them in their finished work. I hear them. Laughing. Talking. Sizing up next steps. Moving ladders. Hanging from the chimney. Kneeling in the corners.

I miss them. I wonder if they miss me. I hope so.

"I am lost in a snowstorm. One of my companions assures me that he can see lights in the distance and that there is a village. But it is only a delusion, which we believe because we choose to do so."
—Tolstoy

CALVING SEASON

There were three distinct reasons I knew I wasn't in a San Francisco restaurant. The single question was which was most important.

The first was the wooden boxes stamped "AMMUNITION" lining the corridor to the dining room. "Dining room" didn't quite fit, unless scarred floors, metal tables, mounted animal heads, and a makeshift corner bar count.

The second was the menu. Printed across the top it said, "We are truly in the Middle of Nowhere," which was the name of the 800 acre "Resort for the Outdoor Enthusiast" surrounded by hundreds more acres of corn and soybeans where we were. A map on the reverse side underscored the claim. No towns in sight. No freeways. The address: Highway WW, Harris, Missouri. The telephone number: 660 794-LOST. Many San Francisco restaurants have names you can't pronounce, much less understand. "The Middle of Nowhere" was in the middle of nowhere. They got that right.

The food choices ran to fried. Fried chicken fingers. Fried spicy pickles. Fried cauliflower. Fried gizzards. Featured specialties—all beef. Roasts. Steaks. Meatloaf and mashed potatoes. Ham and Beans cost $4.00. Mac and cheese $1.50. Many San Francisco restaurants charge those prices for water.

The clinching reason was a practical one. The waiter was wearing a loaded gun. Since we were sitting and he was standing, I was eye to eye with his holster. I'd seen a lot in my life. The move into our current California house was my twenty-sixth relocation. Then there were all the business and holiday travel excursions. This was a new low. Forget the food. Every negative stereotype about guns popped into my head. Ideas are hard to change. My trips to rural Missouri became a high point once I stopped peering through preconceived, rusty biases.

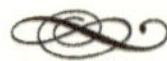

On May 20, 1862, Abraham Lincoln signed the Homestead Act, the federal law that gave applicants up to 160 acres of undeveloped land outside the original thirteen colonies. 1.6 million homesteads were settled, requiring only a simple three-step process. File an application, improve the land, and register a deed. One of those homesteaders was William Clark Ayers, my great-great grandfather.

A Civil War veteran, he built a house high on a northeast Missouri hill overlooking Spring Creek in Sullivan County. There he set about raising three daughters and four sons. One of those sons was my great grandfather, for whom my father was named. Dad left home in 1939. He returned only once the next sixty years.

My sister, in Kansas City on business early in 2000, decided to rent a car and drive the 180 miles north to see the place where our father had grown up but rarely talked about. There she met a half dozen of Dad's cousins, all of whom missed him at their annual September reunions at the Ayers farm—330 of the original 900 acres, the house and two barns, meticulously restored by the wealthiest of them. Her trip was the catalyst he needed.

Thus began a surprising journey of reconnecting with Missouri—

the family left behind, the places that shaped our father, the joy of retracing our roots to a miniature cemetery above a sturdy red barn built by my grandfather in 1911. Among the worn headstones one, barely legible, reads, "W.C. Ayers—December 2, 1813-August 2, 1884."

Charles Movelli is one of our best living plein air artists and teachers. Famous for his town landscapes and coastal view painting, he lives part of the time in Maine. For some years my fall routine has included trips to Missouri and Maine—the first for pleasure, the second for business. Sitting in the middle of nowhere I thought of Movelli. He says, "On the face of it, the easiest of all things should be seeing what we see. In reality, it's the hardest." Loving coastal Maine is easy. His work captures its beauty, energy, vitality. Rural Missouri looks different. Beyond the quiet panoramas is the same vitality…harder to see but there…in the faces, in the hands. When I concentrated I saw a world I grew to love. Not the guns. The people. Art teaches people to see. At least it taught me.

When a cousin expected at the family reunion in the nearest "city"—population 687—was late one year, she explained, "There was a rattlesnake between me and my truck. I had to get my gun." Farmers and ranchers need guns. The more we visited, the more I understood.

Joyce Ayers, the relative with the rattlesnake problem, lived alone on a farm that seemed as isolated as the hunting and shooting range where we had eaten. Widowed early, she raised her family, farmed, and began to paint.

"I always liked drawing and painting. When my husband asked me to paint his bird dog, I was hooked," she said. Her love became a business. "Wildflower Studios" is filled with paintings she sells online, at fairs, in galleries. Her picture of her grandson sitting in a field on a hay bale is in an exhibit at the state capitol. A painter in a tiny corner of Missouri is something else I didn't expect to find. Farmers and ranchers are more than farmers and ranchers. I wonder why I ever thought otherwise.

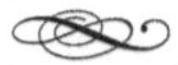

Until painted china has been fired in a kiln it is not complete. The heat matures the mineral colors and binds them to the porcelain. Manipulating kiln heat, which ranges to 1940F degrees, requires learning what happens at different temperatures to different colors, how to stack projects, how fast to heat the chamber. China designs often take as many as five or six firings.

My father bought my first kiln. Opening it after a firing is like opening a package—exciting. When I finish a design in three fires I feel victorious. One December I took a workshop with a well-known painter, the longtime president of the California Association of Porcelain Artists. The subject was holly.

As she demonstrated she said, "This is a one-fire piece." One-fire piece? China is supposed to take multiple firings. The teacher explained, "If you mix paint to a creamier consistency, restrict your palette, work from background to foreground instead of what we normally do, and pay attention to details, one-fire pieces can be lovely."

I was skeptical. That's not what I was taught. Every December when I unwrap the holiday vase I think of the many things I have "unlearned." Unlearned about Missouri. Unlearned about painting. Some pieces take many firings. Some don't. Some mistakes can be fixed. Some need to be wiped off…no matter how long I've worked on them.

A veteran painter in my class would sometimes throw up her hands in frustration, wiping off hours of work. Muttering to herself, she would say, "It's only china." Then she'd plow back in. It was a great deal more than china—it was resilience.

There's a good word for this kind of unlearning—"disenthrall." Mark Stevenson, author of *An Optimist's Tour of the Future*, borrows it from Abraham Lincoln, whose 1862 message to Congress speaks of disenthralling ourselves of "the dogmas of the quiet past" in order to "think anew."

Stevenson's pragmatic attitude about the future doesn't belong exclusively to Silicon Valley, or New York, or Brooklyn, or Los Angeles. I see it in unexpected places. Rural America. Suburban America. Art schools. Craft classes. All trying new materials. New techniques. New ways to achieve outcomes. Stevenson quotes biotech entrepreneur Juan Henriquez, "Attempting to hold on to something by trying to fight against something that humans do best—evolve through culture and technology—is a contradictory and ultimately futile course of action."

I would put it another way. We are always on a path, never at a turning point. We just think we are. My Missouri relatives have weathered a hundred and fifty years of change…one step at a time. Porcelain painters continue to experiment, using advances in chemistry to improve paint, advances in technology to improve kilns.

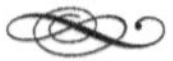

I asked my painting cousin if she was lonely. She paused. "I've lived on farms all my life. The country isn't lonely. It's home. I choose not to live in the past. I'm taking a painting class online from a Canadian artist. I'm learning a lot. Besides, it's spring calving season. New beginnings. And my faith gives me hope."

I will never get used to the menu at the Middle of Nowhere. That's okay. The food may not work, but the people do. People who are complex, self-sufficient, and resilient. It's hard to give up biases—social, political, artistic. I won't give up multiple firing—but I appreciate what single fire can do. I've begun to experiment. I painted a set of one-fire plates based on images from Missouri fields—sunflowers, thistles, wheat. They don't look like the work of people I have studied with. They're my own.

Winslow Homer knew. He said, "When you paint, try to put down exactly what you see. Whatever else you have to offer will come out anyway."

If Lincoln had looked back instead of forward, my ancestors wouldn't have come to Missouri. I'm glad he didn't.

My long journey with art began in the past. I see lights in the future now. It's not the delusion of Tolstoy's village in the snowstorm. It's the luminosity of resilient people—city people and country people.

Art taught me to appreciate both.

"I had rather be on my own farm than be emperor of the world."
—George Washington

"I came to think that art is exactly not what religion is. That it's not about absolutes and it has to do with the condition of being human, which is not ever to be able to deal with absolutes. We live in a world of doubts, a world of uncertainties, a world of ironies."
—Kirk Varnedoe, 1946-2003
Professor of Art, Institute for Advanced Study, Princeton University

OPEN SYSTEMS

The twentieth century saw the birth of a quiet revolution in Western thought. There are challenges to find new ways of thinking and doing in all fields. Those at the end of the Middle Ages and Renaissance didn't know what they were in the middle of because the Modern era had just begun. It is over now, but we can barely see the outlines of a new framework.

What is clear is that instead of a deterministic predict-and-control system, biology's open systems model is here. Gone is the certainty of laws and uniform relations. Alternative patterns and multiple interpretations are the basis for constructing meaning.

John Maeda, President of the Rhode Island School of Design, is a visual artist, designer, computer engineer, and former professor at the Media Lab at the Massachusetts Institute of Technology. He says, "We are learning to look at objects not in isolation, but within the context of everything that surrounds them—how they fit into the entire fabric of society."

Despite the software that makes creativity seem easy, he says, "The truth is, creativity doesn't come easy. It comes hard. It demands discipline and knowledge, and application."

In this turbulent environment it is easy for tiny temporary single-issue groups to form and re-form at high speed, looking for ways to leverage their particular issue. Consider the case of Anton Drexler, a railroad machinist in 1919. He headed a tiny fringe group in Munich. At its first public meeting 111 people attended. The 30-minute speaker: Adolph Hitler.

There are many explanations for Hitler's rise, but thinking of the chaos of non-linear systems, two things are clear: Pressure from outside carries more weight, and positive feedback creates snowball effects. People don't think for themselves.

Few people suggest arts and crafts as preparation for anything relevant in dangerous times. They are. A good example is scientist, artist, and writer David Carroll. Trained at the School of the Museum of Fine Arts in Boston and at Tufts, he is best known, besides winning a MacArthur Foundation "genius" grant in 2006, for the five books he's written and illustrated about turtles, natural history, and his life. *Following the Water* was a 2009 finalist for the National Book Award. The drawings are beautiful, the writing visual, the science compelling.

"What good is it to be alive on earth and never come to know at least one place?" he asks in *Following the Water*. "We don't even try to know it with our senses, much less with our minds and spirits." Carroll was trained to see—parts and wholes. He helps others do the same.

I wasn't thinking of profound shifts in large systems when I began my long affair with arts and crafts. My focus was narrow—home. The more I learned, the more I undertook, the more tools I used, the wider the world became. I saw how elements combine to create unity. By making things. By recognizing the whole is bigger than the parts.

William Maslow said, "If the only tool you have is a hammer, you tend to see every problem as a nail." Arts and crafts gave me many more means to understand, interact, appreciate life. More tools.

It has been a way to gather hopes, plans, colors, shapes. To leave something for the tomorrow we cannot see. A story.

"Once upon a time, there was a home…"

EPILOGUE

My journey with arts and crafts began with uncertainty. It ended in joy.

The joy of learning to:
- Discern
- Begin
- Deconstruct
- Embellish
- Re-imagine
- Vary   (Energy Unbridled)

- Practice
- Reflect
- Adapt
- Bridge
- Devote
- Share   (Etches in Time)

The joy of learning about:
- Design
- Balance
- Focus
- Shape
- Value
- Direction   (Eye Contact)

126

- Movement
- Texture
- Color   (Edging Toward Understanding)

The joy of awareness in:
- Limits
- Space
- Connection
- Resilience
- Systems   (Earthshine)

I found home. It was there all along. It wasn't a place with an address. It was a place in my imagination. I only needed to find it. Arts and crafts gave me some of the tools to bring it to life. I understood at last what John Keats meant:

I am certain of nothing but the holiness of the heart's affections and the truth of imagination—what the imagination seizes as beauty must be truth—whether it existed before or not.

It exists. Look in the night sky when the moon isn't full. It is there, waiting.

Earthshine.

ACKNOWLEDGMENTS

Many influences make any book possible. Many people deserve thanks. This one is no exception. First, the writers and artists quoted, who continue to influence my thinking. Second, teachers who shared their expertise: the Maude Kerns Art Center staff; Terrece Siddoway and Ailene Lew for their mastery of paper design; Ann Apperson for her gift of porcelain instruction; Julaina Kleist-Corwin for bringing art to language; Patricia Marshall for her skill and care in bringing books to life; and to my students, whose creativity made every school project better.

Thanks also for an early opportunity to teach at Eugene's Four Seasons Arts and Crafts Center. The best way to learn is to teach others.

To my father, for buying my first kiln; to my family for their encouragement; to my husband for supporting my efforts—often disruptive, sometimes inconvenient—with love.

Irish novelist and short story writer Elizabeth Bowen says, "Artists, like children, do their best in an atmosphere of affection and encouragement." Special thanks to the Monday writers and Wednesday painters for both.

Finally, to women in American history, who tend to be forgotten. In the early 1900s hundreds of unknown painters lapsed into obscurity because people thought they were unimportant. People were wrong.

To all. Thank you.

Anne Koch
Pleasanton, California
2012

www.ingramcontent.com/pod-product-compliance
Lightning Source LLC
Chambersburg PA
CBHW022059050726
47591CB00002B/609